WAYWARD
CHRISTIAN
SOLDIERS

WAYWARD
CHRISTIAN
SOLDIERS

*Freeing the Gospel from
Political Captivity*

CHARLES MARSH

OXFORD
UNIVERSITY PRESS
2007

OXFORD
UNIVERSITY PRESS

Oxford University Press, Inc., publishes works that further
Oxford University's objective of excellence
in research, scholarship, and education.

Oxford   New York
Auckland   Cape Town   Dar es Salaam   Hong Kong   Karachi
Kuala Lumpur   Madrid   Melbourne   Mexico City   Nairobi
New Delhi   Shanghai   Taipei   Toronto

With offices in
Argentina   Austria   Brazil   Chile   Czech Republic   France   Greece
Guatemala   Hungary   Italy   Japan   Poland   Portugal   Singapore
South Korea   Switzerland   Thailand   Turkey   Ukraine   Vietnam

Published by Oxford University Press, Inc.
198 Madison Avenue, New York, NY 10016
www.oup.com

Oxford is a registered trademark of Oxford University Press

Library of Congress Cataloging-in-Publication Data
Marsh, Charles
Wayward Christian soldiers : freeing the Gospel from political
captivity / Charles Marsh.
p. cm.
Includes bibliographical references and index.
ISBN 978-0-19-530720-7
1. Evangelicalism—United States.   2. Christianity and politics—United States.
I. Title.
BR1642.U5M36 2007
261.70973—dc22   2006038597

1 3 5 7 9 8 6 4 2
Printed in the United States of America
on acid-free paper

For Karen
Henry, Will, and Nan

They shall wander from sea to sea,
and from north to east;
they shall run to and fro, seeking the word of the LORD,
but they shall not find it.

—Amos

ACKNOWLEDGMENTS

I offer my heartfelt thanks to the members of the Virginia Seminar on Lived Theology, Patricia Hampl, Carlos Eire, Mark Gornik, Susan Holman, Charles Mathewes, Alan Jacobs, and Bekah Menning, and to my wonderful colleagues in the Religious Studies Department at the University of Virginia. I am grateful to Joan Gunzelman and the ecumenical community at Ring Lake Ranch in Dubois, Wyoming, as well as to Nancy Brumsted and the retreat ministry of St. John's Episcopal Church in Jackson Hole, where many of these ideas came alive for the first time. I wish to thank the many people who made generous contributions to this book: my wonderful agent, Christy Fletcher, who kept me focused on the essentials; my research assistants, Aurelius Wilson, Ashley Diaz, Sarah Azaransky, and Jacob Goodson; my editor at Oxford University Press, Cynthia Read, for her steady support and laser-sharp insights; my meticulous, collegial copy editors at Oxford, Lelia Mander and Matt Forster; my friends Lauren Winner, Taylor Branch, Wolfgang Huber, and Susan Glisson, for their generosity and inspiration; to my mother and father, Bob and Myra Marsh, for their friendship and unfailing kindness; and the over-the-hill basketball crowd. I am grateful to my wife, Karen Wright Marsh, and to our children Henry, Will, and Nan, and for the time we have been blessed to share; I dedicate this book to them with all my love and affection.

CONTENTS

WAYWARD
CHRISTIAN
SOLDIERS

ON BEING A CHRISTIAN AFTER BUSH

I N A GERMAN CONCENTRATION CAMP in 1944, the theologian, pastor, and Christian martyr Dietrich Bonhoeffer pondered the
future of the church in Germany as it lay in the ruins of a fatal allegiance to Hitler. "The time of words is over," he wrote. "Our
being a Christian today will be limited to two things: prayer and
righteous action."[1] Bonhoeffer believed that the church had so
compromised its witness to Jesus Christ that it was now inca-
pable of "taking the word of reconciliation and redemption to
mankind and the world."[2] The misuse of the language of faith
had corrupted the word; any hope for renewal would need to begin with the humble recognition that God was most certainly
tired of all our talk.

It is time to give Bonhoeffer's meditations a new hearing. With
many other Christians in the United States and many more
abroad, I have watched with horror in recent years as the name
of Jesus has been used to serve national ambitions, strengthen
middle-class values, and justify war. Forgetting the difference

between discipleship and partisanship, the God we have come to trust in these late days is a simulacrum of the holy and righteous God, a domestication of the Christ who comes to humanity from the faraway country of the Trinity. Happily, and, it would appear, with complete indifference to the wisdom and insights of the Christian tradition, we have recast the faith according to our cultural preferences and baptized our prejudices, along with our will to power, in the shallow waters of civic piety. American patriotism has become a cult of self-worship consecrated by court prophets in pin-striped suits. We have too often seized the language of the faith and made it captive to our partisan agendas—and done so with contempt for Scripture, tradition, and the global, ecumenical church.

What is a theologian to do? Perhaps it might now seem appropriate, at a time when evangelical power has begun to wane (at least in the view of some observers), to move forward and try not to worry too much about the consequences of our reckless speech and actions. But much damage has been done, and the theologian—all of us, really—must take stock of the whole colossal wreck of the evangelical witness in America and try to separate the junk from the precious cargo, and then try to rebuild. We dare not walk away from the mess like it is no big deal.

What is a Christian to do? Perhaps the place to start is with the simple conviction that the church of Jesus Christ exists at one and the same time in all peoples, beyond all national boundaries, political, social, or racial, to remember that those who confess Jesus Christ as Lord are quite necessarily and (if you will) ontologically members of the global body of Christ, and that—as Bonhoeffer once said to an ecumenical conference in Denmark after the Nazis had gained control of the German church and nation—"the brothers [and sisters] who make up this church are bound together, through the commandment of the one Lord Christ, whose Word they hear, more inseparably than [people] are bound by all the ties of common history, of blood, of class, and of language."[3]

This book first took shape in my mind as a jeremiad against the conservative Christian elites who, in exchange for political access and power, ransacked the faith and trivialized its convictions. Who could deny that the daily installments of American Christianity—in newspapers, magazines, Web sites, bookstores, and talk shows—have in recent years borne the sad evidence of a church in retreat from the mission of proclaiming hope and forgiveness to the nations? It is as though Christians in the United States consider themselves to be recipients of a special revelation, as if God has whispered eternal secrets in their ears and summoned them to world-historic leadership in the present and future age. Charles Colson, the columnist for *Christianity Today* and former chief of staff to Richard Nixon, called Bush's victory over John Kerry the gift of "Providence" and a "miraculous deliverance." God is "giving us a chance to repent and to restore some moral sanity to American life," said Colson.[4]

Although some opinion makers claim that the 2006 midterm elections chastened evangelical political ambitions, one could also read a different message in the results. The success of the Democratic Party in the midterms—winning the majority of both houses of Congress—served as a sober reminder that evangelicals dare not be complacent in their mission of returning the nation to moral sanity. Of course, this may be a slightly alarmist take on the current situation. Only time will tell. That the situation is now more complicated is beyond dispute. America has become a nation of noisy believers.

W_{AYWARD} *CHRISTIAN SOLDIERS* enters the national debate on faith and politics at a time when leaders of an emerging Christian left have begun holding out the promise of a more comprehensively just and moral account of faith than the narrow agendas of the Christian right. In particular, the success of Jim Wallis's 2005 book, *God's Politics*, introduced many Americans to a vibrant culture of progressive Christianity ready to exert its growing influence over national politics, mobilize the churches around global poverty and AIDS relief, and revitalize the Democratic Party. Nevertheless, this movement to reclaim the soul of politics, refreshing and urgently needed as it is, still, I believe, fails to reckon with the grave and systemic effects of the Christian saturation of the American public square, and with the wide-ranging consequences of this saturation, with the death-by-a-thousand-equivocations of religious language. A period of widespread faith-fatigue is almost certainly on the way. In fact, I am hard pressed to imagine any other explanation than this for the success of Sam Harris's book, *The End of Faith: Religion, Terror, and the Future of Reason*, a polemic against religious belief that revisits the anti-theistic critiques of David Hume, Ludwig Feuerbach, Sigmund Freud, and Friedrich Nietzsche and concludes with the unoriginal observation that religion is an opiate for intellectual scaredy-cats and Christianity "the story of bookish men parsing a collective delusion." This phrase actually comes from Harris's latest, his *Letter to an American Christian*, a slim book that relies heavily upon the sophomoric chortle that there exists no difference between the believer's claim to be in "dialogue with God" and a madman's hunch that his hair dryer bestows the meaning of life.[5] In any case, the presence of the Christian Left at the table with the Christian Right seems to be producing as much cacophony as clarity.

But my book is not about Sam Harris, though Mr. Harris has a lot in common with the Christian Right. The two hurl lumpy dogmatisms at each other like children in a food fight. My book is about Christians in the United States and a truth dishonored. Have Christians forgotten that we are first and foremost reporters of astonishing events, guardians of precious and confounding words? Indeed, I fear we have grown accustomed to speaking of God by speaking of our own needs and preferences in a loud voice, and for the profit and approval that taste so sweet to our lips.

Far more troubling than the evangelical glee over the successes of the Republican majority were the sermons preached in support of the U.S. invasion of Iraq identifying the American plan with the will of God. The war sermons of the fall of 2002 and spring of 2003, delivered in the sanctuaries and worship centers of conservative churches, successfully rallied congregations behind the preemptive attack on Iraq. By the time American troops began bombing Baghdad just before sunrise on March 20, 2003, the collective effort of the religious elites had sanctified the president's decision and convinced the laity that the war was God's will for the nation. A Pew Charitable Trusts poll conducted in April 2003 revealed that an astonishing 87 percent of all white evangelical Christians in the United States supported the invasion.[6] Evangelicals preached for the war, prayed for the war, sang for the war, and offered God's blessings on the war.

"God is pro-war," Jerry Falwell boasted in the title of an essay he wrote in 2004.

SOMETIME AFTER THE PRESIDENT SIGNED off on Operation Iraqi Freedom, I made a remarkable discovery. I had gone to one of my local Christian bookstores to find a Bible for my goddaughter. On a whim, I also decided to look for a Holy Spirit lapel pin, the kind that had always been easy to find in the display case in the front. Many people in my church and in the places where I traveled had been wearing the American flag on their lapel for months now. It seemed like a pretty good time for Christians to put the Spirit back on. But the doves were nowhere in sight. In the place near the front where I once would have found them, I was greeted instead by a full assortment of patriotic accessories—red-white-and-blue ties, bandanas, buttons, handkerchiefs, "I support our troops" ribbons, "God Bless America" gear, and an extraordinary cross and flag bangle with the two images welded together and interlocked. I felt slightly panicked by the new arrangements. I asked the clerk behind the counter where the doves had gone; they had always been so popular in the subculture. The man's response was jarring, although the remark might well be remembered as an apt theological summation of the current religious age. "They're in the back with the other discounted items," he said, nodding in that direction.

I looked around the store. I had not been there for a while, and the whole place looked different. In fact, it looked like a store getting ready for the Fourth of July, although Easter was just weeks away. Next to the cash register was Stephen Mansfield's *The Faith of George W. Bush,* and next to this was David Aikman's *A Man of Faith: The Spiritual Journey of George W. Bush.* On a nearby table, Thomas Freiling's collection, *George W. Bush: On God and Country*, was on display, along with Paul Kengor's *God and George W. Bush* and the president's own book, *A Charge to Keep: My Journey to the White House.*

I have thought of this visit to the Christian bookstore many times in the past several years. I remember the outrage I felt when I saw a photograph in *Time* magazine's 2004 presidential election issue of Christian Coalition activists in Ohio. Two men, both white, and both identified as Coalition members, are holding two crosses aloft. The crosses upon closer inspection appear to be made of balloons twisted together. A friend later told me these balloons are called "thundersticks," which people bang together at sporting events to produce an infernal racket. Across the beam-section of one of the crosses was the "Bush-Cheney" logo, and alongside the president's name—which was positioned exactly where the beams intersect—was the image of an American flag. In the second cross, the president's name appeared in full at the places where Jesus' hands were nailed. My first response when I saw the picture was thinking how much I wished I had a Holy Spirit lapel pin and I could have sent the twisted cross screeching through the air. I then realized I had to write this book.

Imagine a people who stand before the great event of Easter without reverence or humility, a people who simply do not know or (worse) do not care how much is at stake in confessing Jesus Christ as Lord, who sometimes act as if the ideas, words, and images of the faith exist solely for their pleasure, and you would certainly not expect to find a people who also consider themselves to be the most righteous and wholesome in the history of the world, or, as Dr. James Kennedy likes to say, to be "the vice-regents of God."

I fear that the gospel has been humiliated in our time. But if this has happened, it is not a result of changes in the message, or from the machinations of the secularists, nor is it because the post-Enlightenment world has dispensed with the hypothesis of God. The Christian faith has not only endured modernity and post-modernity but has flourished in its new settings. The gospel has been humiliated because those of us entrusted with the mission of proclaiming repentance and salvation to the nations have decided that there are more important things to talk about. We would rather talk about our country, our values, our troops, and our way of life; and although we might think we are paying tribute to God, when we speak of these other things, we are only flattering ourselves. Evangelicals in the United States have tried so hard to become relevant that we have forgotten what it means to be peculiar. But what we need now is not more relevance or more connections; what we need is to experience the gospel again in its strangeness and mystery; to be reminded that the only reliable basis of Christian thinking and action is God's revelation of himself in Jesus Christ, and thus that only God is God.[7] "To be simple," says Bonhoeffer, "is to fix one's eye solely on the simple truth of God at a time when all concepts are being confused, distorted and turned upside-down."[8]

Remember the first commandment: "Thou shalt have no other gods before me" (Exod. 20:3 KJV)? A concrete application of the divine law to our time might well read: God does not need America in order to be God.

IN HIS LETTER TO THE YOUNG CHURCH IN Corinth, Saint Paul spoke of a time in his ministry when "so utterly, unbearably crushed," he despaired of life itself. I think I now understand something of that spiritual despair, and I am surely not alone. In my conversations with church people, ministers, and seminarians around the United States, the question I hear so often is how can Christians begin to rebuild the church's shattered witness after a time of compromise and accommodation? Occasionally I hear Christians describing themselves as "embarrassed," as if they had been observing friends and family feeding gluttonously from a smorgasbord of rich foods. I hear such urgent questions raised as: How can Christians free the gospel from its political captivity? How can we find our way back to simplicity and trust, honesty and straightforwardness?

Consider for a moment the heart of Christian belief. In the glorious prologue to his narrative on the life of Jesus, Saint John said that "the Word became flesh and lived among us, and we have seen his glory . . . full of grace and truth"; "from his fullness, we have all received, grace upon grace" (John 1:14–16). Christians believe that in the incarnation, God spoke a decisive and joyful "Yes," and that this "Yes" secured the ultimate defeat of despair and death. In the new order that Jesus brings—"I am come that they might have life, and that they might have it more abundantly" (John 10:1 KJV)—the "Yes" and "Amen" of God entered into history, and that "Yes" and "Amen" bring hope, light, truth, and peace: the peace that passes all understanding. Christians believe that in Jesus, the last word is not "You are judged" but "You are loved," and thus that Satan's own desperate attempts to be the last word have been defeated. As the Protestant theologian Karl Barth said, "The last word concerning the world of men is not 'Dust thou art and unto dust shalt thou return!' but, 'Because I live, ye shall live also.' "[9] We live with the hope of the resurrection of the dead, and the life of the world to come![10]

What is an evangelical? An evangelical is anyone who memorizes John 3:16 in order to remain mindful of life's basic meaning: "For God so loved the world that he gave his only begotten Son, that whosever believeth in him should not perish but have everlasting life" (KJV). An evangelical is anyone who believes that the Christian gospel—the good news of God's amazing grace poured out for all humanity—is the place where life finds depth and perspective. Saint Matthew describes Jesus as "a great light" that springs out of darkness, light so surprising, so arresting, the light of the world. An evangelical is anyone who has walked out of sin's darkness into the light of Christ. If we call ourselves Christians, it should break our hearts to see that astonishing message cheapened and profaned.

I came of age in the American South in the 1960s, and the moral values shared by most families in the churches of my childhood were deeply interwoven with our culture's hold on white supremacy. The vigilant and quite often neurotic defense that we made of the Southern way of life blinded us not only to the sufferings of African Americans—the victims of our collective self-righteousness—but also to our spiritual arrogance and group pride. We believed that our conception of Christianity and our cherished family values were the most wholesome and pure the world had ever known. Inside a serene delusion, we presumed ourselves to be paragons of virtue, although we rarely lifted a finger to help anyone but our own. It was unsettling to learn sometime in my adolescence that the moral values I inherited as a white southerner were not the marks of true Christian piety. But this was a lesson I needed to learn, for I never would have known the joys of discipleship to Christ had I not reckoned with the fact that my own cultural traditions and tastes had little to do with the gospel.

When Jesus spoke of the family, he had in mind the new community of God. "Who are my mother and my brothers?" he asked one day upon hearing that his family was asking for him. "Here are my mother and my brothers!" Jesus said, pointing to the people gathered around him, who marveled at his words. "Whoever does the will of God is my brother and sister and mother" (Mark 3:33–35). Jesus knew that loyalty to the kingdom of heaven would often require the renunciation of family traditions and habits of culture and custom.

On another occasion, while he was talking with his disciples, Jesus cited a passage from the prophet Micah:

> For I have come to set a man against his father, and a daughter against her mother, and a daughter-in-law against her mother-in-law; and one's foes will be members of one's own household. (Matt. 10:35–36)

Jesus told the disciples that leaving their mothers and fathers was one of the costs of taking up the cross. Cleaving to the family of God meant learning to lose one's life in order to save it, receiving true life and living it abundantly.

As for its current popular usage, we should not forget that the word "values" is rooted in economics and has nothing to do with the formation of Christian disciples. A value is the purchasing power of a commodity, the quality on which utility and worth depend, "the power of a commodity to purchase others," as the *Oxford English Dictionary* states. A moral value in contemporary American English might be called the power to purchase votes from evangelical Christians.[11]

In his Epistle to the Galatians, Saint Paul wrote that "the works of the flesh" are seen in dissension, envy, idolatry, drunkenness, anger, and carousing; but the "fruit of the Spirit" is love, joy, peace, patience, kindness, generosity, faithfulness, gentleness, and self-control. Those who live by the Spirit will also be guided by the Spirit. According to Paul, genuine righteousness begins with the humble recognition that fellowship with God is not a possession over which we may boast, nor is it any kind of entitlement or inherited virtue, and surely not a weapon to deploy in the culture wars of the age. Righteousness takes shape in single-minded commitment to Jesus and reveals its authenticity in the flowering of love, joy, peace, patience, kindness, generosity, faithfulness, gentleness, and self-control.

On the first anniversary of the terrorist attacks of September 11, 2001, President Bush's speechwriters chose Ellis Island and the scenic backdrop of New York Harbor as the location for his televised address to the nation. In his speech that night, the president described the ideal of America as "the hope of all mankind," the "cause of human dignity; freedom guarded by conscience and guarded by peace." This hope, he told us, had drawn millions to the harbor in search of freedom and dignity. "That hope still lights our way," he continued. "And the light shines in the darkness. And the darkness will not overcome it."

Writing in *The New Statesman* a week later, Mark Dowd noted that the president and his writers had borrowed (Dowd said "pirated") the prologue to the Fourth Gospel, "perhaps the most eloquent and philosophically significant words in the Gospel narratives."[12] The conservative Christian community indulged the president his rhetorical play on the "word made flesh," and no one raised objections: the president's approval was soaring into the high seventies at the time, and America needed consoling words from its leaders. Still, in his speech Bush had ventured to propose an idea no less audacious than the identification of the United States with Christian revelation. The blurring of this difference was a sign of greater dangers to come. Why not borrow other precious sources as well, like the old Protestant hymn, "There Is Power in the Blood," to talk about "the wonderworking power" of the American people? The sacrificial blood of the lamb shed for the sins of the world was not quite what the times required.

Have we in the Christian community forgotten that we serve a God who really *is*, who sees and hears and shares our sorrows, and a God who listens with favor to the victim and the oppressed; that the God we confess to be the true and living God is a God who stands in our midst?

"For he shall deliver the needy when he crieth; the poor also, and him that hath no helper," the psalmist says (Ps. 72:12 KJV). "Evening, and morning, and at noon, will I pray, and cry aloud: and he shall hear my voice" (Ps. 55:17 KJV). The God we confess to be true is a living God who listens. "God heard their groaning. . . . and God took notice of them," the book of Exodus says (2:23–25).[13] God hears the cries of men and women killed, maimed, and dispossessed, of orphaned, battered, and forgotten children, of all those crushed by violence, famine, and failure. God hears, and God is not silent. The reformer Martin Luther once said that the cries of the suffering and the sighs of despair are the cries and sighs of the Holy Spirit, resounding throughout all of heaven so loudly that the angels listen with rapt attention.[14] "He that is of God heareth God's words," writes Saint John in his gospel, "ye therefore hear them not, because ye are not of God" (John 8:47 KJV). But are we today listening to the groans of broken creation and to the cries and protests of the suffering, and are we listening to God, who hears these lamentations and makes them his own?

Franklin Graham boasted that the American invasion of Iraq opened up exciting new opportunities for missions to non-Christian Arabs. But this is not what the Hebrew prophets or the Christian teachers mean by righteousness and discipleship. In fact, this grotesque notion—that preemptive war and the destruction of innocent life pave the way for the preaching of the good news—strikes me as a mockery of the cross and a betrayal of the Christian's baptism into the body of Christ. "Father, forgive them for they know not what they do," Jesus said in the hour of his greatest agony. To be baptized in the name of the Father, Son, and Holy Spirit means that we are brought into this new reality through this rite of salvation.

On the other hand, if Franklin Graham speaks truthfully of the Christian faith and its mission in the world—as many evangelicals seem to believe—then we should have none of it. We should rather join the ranks of the righteous unbelievers and big-hearted humanists who rage against cruelty and oppression with the intensity of people who live fully in this world. I am certain that it would be better for Christians to stand in solidarity with compassionate atheists and agnostics, firmly resolved against injustice and cruelty, than to sing "Amazing Grace" with the heroic masses who cannot tell the difference between the cross and the flag. The Jesus who storms into Baghdad behind the wheels of a Humvee is not the Jesus of the gospel.

And while we are on the subject, may I please ask a favor of the decent men and women who edit the magazine *Christianity Today*? The next time Franklin Graham utters a remark so completely contrary to the spirit of Christ, please denounce it with the same clarity that your columnists have brought to their criticisms of Bishop Spong's heterodox views, Bill Clinton's lechery, or Mark Felt's deathbed revelation that he was Watergate's Deep Throat. Please denounce it with the same clarity that the Latin American churches brought to their "Communicado de la Fraternidad Teológica Latinoaméricana sobre la guerra," when they resolved that "the havoc wreaked by two 'Christian' nations [the United States and England] would invalidate the proclamation of the gospel in cultures whose voices and contributions we have not yet listened to nor appreciated."[15] As we shall see, this was one of the many global evangelical statements against the war—declarations against the war by evangelicals outside the United States—ignored by the mainline American and religious media.[16]

If only holiness were measured by the volume of our incessant chatter. We would then be universally praised as the most holy nation on earth. But in our fretful, theatrical piety, we have come to mistake noisiness for holiness, and we have presumed to know, with a clarity and certitude that not even the angels dare claim, the divine will for the world. We have organized our needs with the confidence that God is on our side, now and always, whether we feed the poor or corral them into sweltering, subterranean ghettos. The demands of scripture and tradition, the study of Christian doctrine, and the catechisms of the faith have been abandoned for pleasurable technologies and relevant guidebooks. No wonder we have no qualms about mining the faith for sound bites.

On repentance, the Bible admonishes a broken and contrite heart, and the honesty to admit that it is we, the self-righteous and the proud, and not all those wicked others—the pagans, evolutionists, Muslims, unchristian (and Christian) homosexuals, the liberal media, the ACLU, the Dixie Chicks, and the gangsta rappers, or as Jerry Falwell once ranted, "Hollywood, Springsteen, Affleck, Baldwin . . . billionaire George Soros and his ilk, all the 527s, most of the national print and broadcast media, the gays and lesbians, the abortionists, the entire liberal establishment . . . and about $2 billion of hate-inspired media and campaign expenditures"—it is not the usual (and unusual!) suspects who have profaned the gospel of Jesus Christ in our time.[17] The speech writers and the court prophets can plunder the Christian scripture and tradition for whatever political benefits they can get, but at some point near the end of this perilous journey—and aren't we there yet?—the prophets and the pundits, and each of us complicit in the partisan captivity of the gospel, must reckon with the inescapable fact that in our promiscuous talk we have humiliated the word of God.[18]

Repentance means critical self-examination and steadfast prayer, the chastened wisdom of the person who pleads, "create in me a clean heart, O God, and put a new and right spirit within me" (Ps. 51:10). There is no other way forward.

WHAT DOES IT MEAN FOR CHRISTIANS in North America to trust in the Lord with their hearts and minds, as the Proverbs instruct, and to acknowledge him in all their ways, leaning not on their own understanding? The Hebrew prophet Amos delivers a difficult message. To a nation filled with intense religious fervor, Amos says, you are not the holy people you imagine ourselves to be. Though the land is filled with festivals and assemblies, songs and melodies, and with so much pious talk, these are not sounds and sights that are pleasing to the Lord. These are not what the

Lord requires. "Take away from me the noise of your songs," Amos says, "you [who] have turned justice into poison" (Amos 5:23; 6:12 NASB). No peace or solitude will be found in a nation that "abhor him who speaks with integrity" (5:10). God desires instead the melodious sounds of justice "rolling down like waters" and righteousness like "an ever-flowing stream" (5:24); yet what God hears is the din of self-praise. The costs of disobedience are great. In some of the most disturbing verses of the Bible, Amos warns of a famine of the word, a famine more devastating than any "famine of bread" or "thirst for water." He warns of a famine "of hearing the words of the LORD" (Amos 8:11).

> They shall wander from sea to sea, and from north to east;
> they shall run to and fro, seeking the word of the LORD,
> but they shall not find it. (Amos 8:12)

Amidst the clamor of the religious nation, amidst all the self-serving and pious chatter, it will become difficult to hear the roaring Lion of Zion.

Learning to trust in the Lord with all our hearts and minds means we must begin again with God. It means that we must learn how to walk along the Lord's narrow path, and thus to recognize that the battle-scorched highways of our personal ambitions and agendas lead somewhere quite different than to grace and peace. "Be still and know that I am God," the psalmist writes. Dietrich Bonhoeffer, in his classic work on Christian community, *Life Together*, spoke of a silence "before the Word," a silence that stands "under the Word," and a silence that "comes out of the Word." He affirmed the wisdom of the psalmist, the importance of a listening silence. The Christian who cannot be still and silent, Bonhoeffer said, will only bring chaos to the Christian community.

After all the talk and the noise, it is time for Christians in the United States to enter a season of quietness, being still, and learning to wait on God (perhaps for the first time). This will not be easy for us. The armies of the right are in full battle mode, and the air is filled with the sounds of clanking armor. But our throats are parched, and our minds are running in panic. The earth is shrinking fast. All Christian speaking, thinking, and organizing must proceed in a spirit of lament. In this quieter season, we must learn again to behold the holiness and majesty of God; we must abide for awhile with God in a quietness that brings "purification, clarification, and concentration upon the essential thing."[19] Listen to the words of the old eucharistic hymn, "Let all mortal flesh keep silence."

Dietrich Bonhoeffer wrote *Life Together* during the years when he directed an illegal seminary in the North German village of Finkenwalde. The seminary's mission was to train pastors in the Confessing Church, a reform movement that opposed the nazified German Evangelical Church. Being still before the word in a time of enormous historical and ecclesial crisis was surely no invitation to idleness or indifference; it was in fact a call to discernment and responsible action. For in such stillness, our perceptions of life would be transformed by the renewing vision of God. And only in such stillness will Christians be able to recover the reverence and respect that inspires righteous action. Above all, though, we wait before the word so that God might be glorified and his beauty beheld anew.

"Are we still of any use?" Bonhoeffer asked shortly before his arrest on charges of treason.[20] I might also ask: Are theologians still of any use? If we are, it will only be if we have remained honest about our peculiar purposes and then had the courage to take the situation upon us for the sake of the truth of God.[21] Theology must seek to free the language of its current lies so that the word of God can be heard again, for the word has become almost impossible to hear in our nation. The prophet Isaiah says, "In returning and rest shall ye be saved; in quietness and in confidence shall be your strength" (Isa. 30:15 KJV).

The theologian should also be about the business of reminding the church that the sole basis of its existence is the decisive and historically real event of the Son of God born, crucified, buried, and resurrected as man for all humanity.[22] We should remind the church that its language and its proclamations are gifts and deposits of divine revelation, and not our own possessions. We should remind the church that its speaking and its witness are meant to bring glory to God, and to serve always and everywhere as sign posts towards that greater righteousness, that its life is lived solely from the gospel, in a common and universally affirmed relationship to the word of God, in the fellowship of the Holy Spirit, and in the knowledge that the kingdom of God has broken into time and history in the great event of Jesus Christ. We should remind the church that its mission in the world is to proclaim the good news of God's love to all the nations, for this is indeed the mission of every church in every nation.

Are we still of any use? Bonhoeffer's reply might well be taken as the hope and the challenge of the present age: "We have been silent witnesses of evil deeds; we have been drenched by many storms; we have learnt the arts of equivocation and pretence; experience has made us suspicious of others and kept us from being truthful and open; intolerable conflicts have worn us down and even made us cynical. Are we still of any use? What we shall need is not geniuses, or cynics, or misanthropes, or clever tacticians, but plain, honest, straightforward people. Will our inward power of resistance be strong enough, and our honesty with ourselves remorseless enough, for us to find our way back to simplicity and straightforwardness?"[23]

My prayer is that this book will help Christians learn to live in truth and show the world through their vocations, habits, and testimonies that the love of God is the peace the world longs for, the healing we so desperately need. Beyond jeremiad and lament, the following meditations and analyses move towards an edifying purpose. I wish to remind my brothers and sisters in Christ—and non-Christians as well, who often mistake, understandably, our bad habits for the message itself—of what it means to confess Christ as Lord and Savior, in order that Christians in the United States might reaffirm the simple fact, amidst all the noise and confusion, that to call oneself a follower of Jesus means to live according to a different standard than political loyalty or nationhood.

Chapter One

THE EVANGELICAL MOMENT

T HE YEARS 2000–2006 MARKED the full ascent of American evangelicals to political prominence and influence. We certainly did come a long way from the time when Francis Schaeffer summoned us in *A Christian Manifesto* to engage the political structures and "roll back the other total entity"—by which he meant defeating secular, liberal culture and its "material-energy, chance world view."[1] Francis Schaeffer was the Presbyterian minister and popular writer who, in the early 1960s, with his wife, Edith Schaeffer, herself a respected evangelical writer, founded the L'Abri community ("l'abri" meaning "the shelter" in French) in a farming village in the Swiss Alps.

Over the next decade, thousands of American evangelicals traveled to Huemoz, Switzerland, to attend his lectures; even more came to hear Schaeffer speak during one of his tours of the United States, where his critique of secular culture eventually captured the attention of the first wave of conservative Christians that formed the core of the Moral Majority. The religious elites and opinion makers who brought George W. Bush to the White House often speak of Francis Schaeffer as a major catalyst of their success.[2] The conservative writer and publisher Marvin Olasky, whose book *The Tragedy of American Compassion* influenced the president's thinking on faith-based policies, explained: "Who's the major figure behind the election and re-election of George W. Bush? On one level, the visionary Karl Rove. At a deeper level, a theologian most Americans have never heard of: Francis Schaeffer, who 50 years ago this month founded an evangelistic haven in Switzerland, L'Abri."[3] Schaeffer's importance in the conservative movement has been noted by Charles Colson, Cal Thomas, Richard Land, Ralph Reed, and many others shapers of evangelical opinion.

Schaeffer's main theme, hammered home in nearly every lecture, book, and conversation, was that the human race, divorced from historic Christianity (revealed, reformational Christianity), was left with two options: escape into an unreality that produces mysticism or descend into a nihilism that reduces persons to machines.[4] Schaeffer's writings encouraged the new evangelicals to understand and to engage intellectual culture, and this was a welcome note to many who had been warned by preachers and Sunday-school teachers to avoid contact with the secular world, or at least to approach it with caution. Yet while Schaeffer inspired a generation of evangelical intellectuals to think and read more freely, he also inspired an emerging network of conservative activists to organize, mobilize, and take back the government.

By the late 1970s Schaeffer had begun entertaining ambitious plans for the political and policy implications of his writings on the secularization of the West. By the time he penned his rousing *Christian Manifesto* in 1981, he had thrown off the mantle of evan-

gelist to the counter-culture and embraced the new role of theological guru to the Christian Right. It excited Schaeffer greatly to
see his writings—more than a dozen slender volumes on the decline of the " great Western Christian consensus"—give momen-
tum to a mass movement seeking to reclaim lost values from a
godless culture.

The *Christian Manifesto* was a clarion call to a marginal people; evangelicals must prepare themselves for the coming culture
wars. "We must understand that there is going to be a battle every
step of the way," Schaeffer wrote. "[The secular humanists] are
determined that what they have gained will not be rolled back.
But it is our task to use the open window to try to change that direction at this very late hour."[5] Schaeffer encouraged evangelicals to organize and mobilize around the threatened moral
foundations of the Christian West and to take to the courts, the
Congress, and the streets as the times required. "We must press
on, hoping, praying, and working," he said, "that indeed the window can stay open and the total entity will be pressed back rather
than the whole thing ending only in words."[6] Schaeffer rendered
judgment against secular humanism in all its godless forms, sum-
moning the conservative churches to swift and decisive action.
He told his followers that to rest content in salvation would be
their undoing. In fact, it was nothing less than the undoing of civilization. They must understand the logic and "flow" of secular
humanism with maximum fluency, and they must then attack its
presuppositions and overwhelm its deceptions.

SCHAEFFER'S VISION OF EVANGELICAL CHRISTIANITY differs in significant ways from the other main influence on the contemporary

evangelical movement. I speak here of John Stott, the revered Anglican evangelical priest and writer whom Billy Graham once called the "most respected clergyman in the world today."[7] Many historians regard the Lausanne Covenant of 1974, which Stott helped draft, as the most important milestone in the evangelical movement's history. Signed by 2,300 evangelical leaders from 150 countries, the Covenant pledged ultimate loyalty to the Great Commission, the evangelistic mandate of Jesus, given in the Gospel of Saint Matthew to "go and make disciples in all the nations."[8] Convened by Billy Graham and led by Stott, the signatories affirmed the global character of the Christian faith and the belief that "the church is the community of God's people rather than an institution, and must not be identified with any particular culture, social or political system, or human ideology."[9] Responding to the conference theme, "Let the Earth Hear His Voice," the signers of the Covenant further affirmed their conviction that "the gospel is God's good news for the whole world." A church that preaches the cross "must itself be marked by the cross."

Although Francis Schaeffer took part in the 1974 International Congress in Lausanne, he would later criticize the Covenant in his book *The Great Evangelical Disaster* as an example of the "widely accepted existential methodology" afflicting the modern church. Schaeffer complained that the Covenant demurred on the inerrancy of the Bible, the belief that the Bible was literally true in every claim and description—including all historical and scientific parts—thus the Lausanne Covenant was marred by "relativism" and the invidious effects of the "new neo-orthodoxy."[10] In fact, the Covenant offers a robust endorsement of Scripture's full reliability as revealed truth: "We affirm the divine inspiration,

truthfulness and authority of both Old and New Testament Scriptures in their entirety as the only written word of God, without
error in all that it affirms, and the only infallible rule of faith and
practice." But that wasn't enough to satisfy Schaeffer. "Inerrancy"
would soon become the battle cry in the emerging Christian
Right's assault on the "amoral thought-forms of our culture," such
forms as progressive social policies, ecumenism, religious doubt,
and any other idea deemed liberal, humanistic, or antagonistic to
strict formulations of "God's absolutes."

Schaeffer's call to political action on behalf of a church under
siege stands in sharp contrast to the Lausanne Covenant. The
Covenant is a Christ-centered manifesto of evangelical passion
free of religious paranoia; it sees the whole world in the embrace
of "God's cosmic purpose" and the church as the community that
proclaims God's purpose to the nations. No doubt people from
other religious traditions, as well as many liberal Christians, might
regard that embrace as a suffocating hug; but Lausanne's affirmations were made in the spirit of gentle persuasion, in service
to truth and mercy, and with a vision of shalom for all the earth.
Lausanne gave voice to an evangelical internationalism that
linked the ancient church's theological orthodoxy and the Reformation doctrine of justification by faith with the twentieth century's Universal Declaration of Human Rights, drafted in 1948
by the General Commission of the United Nations, which the
Lausanne signers explicitly endorsed.

In his 1978 book, *Christian Counter-Culture*, an eloquent exposition of the Sermon on the Mount, Stott spoke of the moral shape of
the Christian life as an alternative lifestyle to the dehumanizing
patterns of the world. "[The] values and standards of Jesus are in
direct conflict with the commonly accepted values and standards of

the world," he wrote.[11] The world prefers the rich man to the poor, the world prefers the "happy-go-lucky and carefree" to the person who laments the brokenness of the human condition. The world prefers the Machiavellian schemer, who attains his ends by any devious means, to the "pure in heart," who refuses to compromise his integrity—the popular and the trendy to those willing to suffer persecution and endure hardship.[12] The followers of Jesus are meant to live according to a different standard.[13] Living in the light of the resurrection and filled with the renewing energies of the Holy Spirit, Christians live as a people who have been called out of old habits and prejudices, as citizens of the new kingdom. They are meant to exemplify compassionate and Christ-centered attitudes towards money, ethics, careers, lifestyles, relationships, and social practices. Christians must then live so as to nurture the authenticity of their witness to the kingdom of God, marked by the genuineness of their love and the clarity of their compassion and generosity.

Sadly, JOHN STOTT'S EVER-SO-MONKISH RULE for counter-cultural evangelicals proved no match for Schaeffer's exhilarating battle cry against the secular hordes overpopulating the public square. At least for most members of the generation of culturally marginalized conservatives, Schaeffer's call proved irresistible. Marginal no longer, by the year 2000 evangelicals had gained leadership in both houses of Congress and were presiding over influential lobbying and consulting firms, preaching at political rallies, writing the president's speeches—and, indeed, occupying the White House itself. In the decades since Crossway Books published Schaeffer's *Christian Manifesto*, evangelical Christians in the

United States became the nation's most powerful political constituency. They will now even look their interlocutors straight in the eye and introduce themselves as the "vice-regents of God."

But—to ask once again and not for the last time—what are the consequences of our Faustian bargain for access and power? I have no doubt that most evangelicals seek to be ambassadors of God's grace and are saddened to realize how their loyalties have become corrupted. Lacking the theological tools to discern the false gods, or at least the humility to interrogate our own motives, I fear we have unwittingly taken the word of God captive and incarcerated it in partisan gulags. American evangelicals have resolved to serve a political agenda with the passion we once gave to personal soul-winning, Bible study, the disciplines of Christian holiness, and worship. We have done so at the cost of cheapening our mission to proclaim the love of God for all nations, which is the obligation of every church in every nation; we have done so by compromising our commitment to the crucified and resurrected Christ, and at the cost of retreating from the shattering truth of the first commandment: "Thou shalt have no other gods before me."

There is no easy way of saying this. Fancying ourselves to be the global caretakers of Christian truth, if not of all truth, we have turned God into an appendage of the American way of life, acted with utter contempt toward the global evangelical and ecumenical church, and at times even presumed that the military powers of our nation act in vicarious representation of Jesus Christ the Lord. By aligning ourselves with political slogans and cultural prejudices, the Christian faith may have gained a certain relevance in our time, but it has achieved this at too great a cost. We really have only ourselves to blame for the spiritual condition of a nation in which the truth of God has become almost impossible to hear. (Can anyone imagine a greater offense to the spirit of Lausanne, and to the gospel of Jesus Christ, than the boast that American warriors in Iraq are helping usher in a new missionary era?[14])

WHAT IS THE GOSPEL, the good news that Christians are invited to proclaim? The gospel is the announcement of the coming of Jesus Christ to save fallen humanity, to reconcile all people with God, and to redeem creation. The Greek term *euangelion*, from which the word "gospel" is derived, is used in the New Testament simply to mean all the gifts that Christ brings. Saint Mark begins his briskly paced narrative of the life of Jesus with the words, "The beginning of the gospel of Jesus Christ, the Son of God." Here, *euangelion* means "the good news which tells about Jesus Christ."[15] Jesus announces the glad tidings of the kingdom of God to the whole world, and to the poor in particular. Jesus saves, liberates, forgives, heals, and loves. He shows us new life; he is new life.

The Hebrew derivative of euangelion is the verb *bśr*, which means "to proclaim a glad and joyful message," as when King David was told by his watchman that the messenger running alone in the distance was on his way to deliver good news (1 Kings 1:42; Jer. 20:15; 2 Sam. 18:26). In the book of Isaiah, the verb *bśr* is used to affirm the sovereignty of God over all creation and history, as we read in chapter 52:

> How beautiful upon the mountains
> are the feet of the messenger who
> announces peace,

> who brings good news,
>> who announces salvation,
>> who says to Zion, "Your God
>> reigns" (52:7–10)

When we turn to early Christian literature, we are struck by the fact that outside of its use in the Christian community, the Greek word euangelion rarely conveys the sense of glad tidings or messages of hope.[16] The poet Homer uses the word in the *Odyssey* (xiv, 152) but in reference to the reward offered a messenger, not to the message itself, and this same sense of the word is found in ancient Greek (Attic), as a sacrifice or offering of thanksgiving made on behalf of a good report. On the other hand, the New Testament writings of Matthew, Mark, Luke, and John are so brimming with "glad tidings" that the early apostolic fathers came to speak of these four books as the "gospel" of Jesus Christ (Didache 8:2; 2 Clement 8:5). In liturgical churches, before the reading of the "gospel," each member of the congregation makes the sign of the cross with the thumb, first above the eyes to open the mind to the word, then on the lips to mark the beauty of the word, and then on the chest, to seal the heart with the word of the Lord.

In his letters to new Christian communities, Paul explains that he was "entrusted with the gospel" (Gal. 2:7) in his ministry of evangelism and theological exposition; he was called "according to the grace of God" (1 Cor. 3:10) to proclaim the good news "so that the cross of Christ might not be emptied of its power" (1:17). The word "gospel" appears more than sixty times in his letters. Proclaiming the gospel does not give the believer the individual right to boast in the righteousness of God; it is rather an expression of gratitude to God for the gift of salvation. Paul says that we are obedient to God when we preach the gospel in the power of the Spirit and in the company of the saints, and thus when we honor the trust God has placed in us as witnesses to his word. The only theological term found more in the letters of Saint Paul than euangelion is *charis*, or grace. "Grace" names the unconditional love of God given freely to all people, a love big enough to embrace the whole world.

The gospel is not then bound to any nation, tribe, or way of life, but is unique to the way God reveals himself in Jesus Christ, which is to say, unique to the "gospel of our Lord Jesus" (2 Thess. 1:8). We hear of "the gospel of the glory of the blessed God" (1 Tim. 1:11 ASV), "the gospel of his Son" (Rom. 1:9 ASV), "the gospel of the glory of Christ" (2 Cor. 4:4 ASV), "the gospel of your salvation" (Eph. 1:13 ASV), and the "word of truth" (Col. 1:5; Eph. 1:13 ASV). The gospel is "free of charge," and because it is free, it must be preserved in its freedom by those entrusted with its proclamation, those who profess Jesus Christ as Lord.[17] "Therefore, my dear friends, flee from the worship of idols" (1 Cor. 10:14). Paul stresses the absolute urgency of communicating the gospel in a way that honors this trust in word and in deed and thus sings the song of God's salvation rather than a song of self-praise.

WHAT IS THE PURPOSE OF LIFE? The purpose of life is to love God, to enjoy God, and to strive to bring glory to God. Saint Paul is so intent on proclaiming the gospel in truth that he instructs ministers and evangelists to "get their own living by the gospel" (1 Cor. 9:14); by so doing, Paul believes, they will remain free from the temptation to accommodate the good news to the expectations and tastes of benefactors. Saint Augustine once said the apostles of Christ teach us that the gospel must always be preached "by love" and not "by occasion." The love of Christ is a living power, which transforms the nature of all things, revealing their ultimate meaning. The apostles "speak not with the mouth only," Augustine said; rather "they pour out that of which they are full; they preach peace, and they have peace."[18]

The gospel changes everything. The gospel announces the glad tidings that Jesus has broken the barricades of heaven and unleashed love everlasting. "Grace, mercy, and peace will be with us, from God the Father, and from the Lord Jesus Christ, the Son of the Father, in truth and love," we read in the Second Letter of John (1:3). Jesus shows us new life; Jesus is new life. He alone traversed the vast distances to bring us the glorious news of God's saving love.

In the Gospel of Matthew we read that the kingdom of heaven is like a person traveling into a far country. In a lonesome land, Jesus gathers by his side a company of friends; the new world he reveals is beautiful and strange.

Jesus is the man who "burns, burns, burns, like the yellow roman candle" but does not burn out: the one who baptizes with the Holy Spirit and with fire, who himself asks to be baptized, receiving the dove-blessing of the Spirit, sent by the Father in love.[19] Jesus looks upon the kingdoms of the world and their splendor but chooses not to possess them, although he is tempted. He knows the price of possession, the worship of the anti-God, the bondage of self-deception. But instead he proclaims the theme of passionate Jewish monotheism: "Worship the Lord your God, and serve him only."

Jesus is a man in movement but not in flight. His movement is the irradiation of stillness, the dance that is the still point. He

calls disciples to journey with him through the villages of
Galilee. He loves his disciples, and they love him, but he loves
them as they are. He does not ask his disciples to be more than
themselves, except in their straightforward devotion to the truth
he proclaims. He will not consume their attention; he directs it to
others, especially the broken and the downcast, the sick and the
afflicted, those who are lost and lonely, welcoming them to the
new order of his love. He announces the good news of the kingdom of God, and he cures every disease and illness. He sojourns
through towns and villages in a life of joyful abandon, trusting
fully in God and in himself. The crowds gather in amazement.

Jesus speaks of a different order than the old ordeal. He invites people into the fellowship of his love, into this kingdom of
heaven, although this kingdom cannot be gained through the ordinary means of avarice and aggression. The community of Jesus
illuminates the true history of the world, the world as it is meant
to be experienced in the great creation dream. The poor in spirit,
those who mourn, those who hunger and thirst for righteousness,
the merciful, the poor in heart, the peacemakers, those who are
persecuted for righteousness, and those who love their enemies,
these are the "children of the Father" (Matt. 5:45).

Jesus surprises his followers, and his critics too, by his lack of
interest in formal piety and the conventional appearances of holiness. He regards the fawning theatrical piety of the religious
elite as pretense and folly. When you give to the poor, you should
do so quietly. When you pray, go into your room and pray to the
Father in secret. Remember that it is the hypocrite who rewards
his own good works with trumpets and clanging bells, who prays
in the street with an eye on his admirers while heaping empty
words on himself. Jesus is drawn to men and women ready to live

in word and truth. The day is their daily bread, and they seek to do the will of God on earth as it is in heaven. Jesus tells his followers not to worry about food or clothing, for if God clothes the lilies of the field with such precise splendor, he will not forget his own children. Those who pick up their cross and follow have no need to worry about all that tomorrow will bring, and in any case tomorrow will certainly bring worries, but the kingdom of God remains in their midst, today and every day.

"Is there anyone among you who, if your child asks for bread, will give a stone? Or if the child asks for a fish, will give a snake? If you then, who are evil, know how to give good gifts to your children, how much more will your Father in heaven give good things to those who ask him!" (Matt. 7:11). If his children forgive others their trespasses, the Father in heaven will forgive them their own.

The earth finds its fulfillment in a heavenly source, and therein it is able to be the earth, the earth that God made, the earth on which Jesus walks. "Give us this day our daily bread," he prays, "on earth as it is in heaven" (Matt. 6:11, 10).

If his children forgive others their trespasses, the Father in heaven will forgive them. The children of the Father are people who trust in God's promises to bless.[20]

Jesus tells the crowds that the gate leading to righteousness is narrow and the first step is hard. But the narrow way leads to the place of their deepest longings; there is light and beauty in the open spaces of grace. The first step changes everything. And still there will be few who enter.

You will know my children by their fruit, Jesus says, for not everyone who calls on the name of the Lord and clothes himself in righteousness shall be called a child of God. It will, in fact, be easier to please the crowds mingling in the town square or even to cast out demons and perform powerful deeds than to find the patience and humility to build a house on solid rock. The thing that matters most is the simple presence of his company, abiding with Jesus in the fullness of his love.

It often perplexes Jesus that the disciples think they need more.

"Why are you afraid, you of little faith?" (Matt. 8:26)

"I desire mercy, not sacrifice" (Matt. 9:13).

"I have come to call not the righteous but sinners" (Matt. 9:13).

"Those who find their life will lose it, and those who lose their life for my sake will find it" (Matt. 10:39).

Jesus journeys through cities and villages, teaching in the synagogues, in the streets and abandoned places, preaching the good news of the kingdom, healing the sick. He sees the crowds and is moved to compassion, for they appear to him as sheep without a shepherd. He knows their hearts' longing and the confusion of their wills, the chaos of the human condition. He soothes the blistered soul, befriends the lonely and the broken. He brings healing to the blind and the lame, the leper and the deaf. The poor stand in his favor. He offers rest to the weary. To the powerful men who lay claim to him as their own, but who do not repent and show mercy, he speaks a word of judgment. "Did you want to be raised as high as heaven?" he asks the proud citizens of Capernaum (Matt. 11:23 NJB). "No, you will be brought down to Hades" (Matt. 11:23).

Yet the judgment he pronounces becomes the judgment he bears in the suffering of the cross. This is the judgment that leaves no man or woman innocent, and yet it is a judgment for which Jesus comes to stand in our place. He bears the sins of the world so that the world might have life and life more abundantly; he relieves us of the burden of sin and guilt. This is all such good news, such amazing grace.

IN THE MONTHS BEFORE THE SECOND IRAQ WAR BEGAN, the American ambassador to Germany was asked by the bishop planning the event to read a passage from the Gospel of Matthew in a commemorative service for Dietrich Bonhoeffer. As a result of his activities as a member of the German resistance, Bonhoeffer had been executed by the Nazis in 1945. The ambassador, a well-known evangelical Christian and frequent guest at the National Prayer Breakfast, thanked the German bishop for the invitation but declined. The passage was from the Sermon on the Mount, Jesus' admonition to "bless those who curse you and pray for those who spitefully use you and persecute you." The Sermon on the Mount had been the inspiration for Bonhoeffer's most widely read book, *The Cost of Discipleship*, in which he wrote, "The love of our enemies takes us along the way of the cross and into the fellowship of the Crucified."[21] Sadly, the American ambassador found himself turning down the invitation to read the gospel out of respect for the evangelical president's mission in Iraq.

Did the decision trouble the ambassador? I truly hope that it did. By all reports, he is a kind and decent man. The German bishop regarded him as sympathetic and congenial. Still, the ambassador's decision did not trouble him so much that he was suddenly overcome with regret, and then, with a clear sense of his greater calling, changed his mind, threw political caution to the wind, and read the Sermon on the Mount to those gathered at the Berliner Dom.

US Ambassador declined to read Gospel

did not

could have read later

But how I wish he had

But how I wish he had. How I wish he had exclaimed, "Of course, I will read from the Sermon on the Mount. I have no other choice. The refusal to read would amount to a renunciation of my faith, and I can never allow my service to the nation to compromise my loyalty to Jesus Christ." How heartening it would have been had the American ambassador declared, "Give me the gospel. I cannot stand before God otherwise."

Shuld Luvd

There was once a time when an evangelical's decision to compromise his faith for access and power would have been unthinkable. Jesus said in the Garden of Gethsemane that the same world that had turned its back on him would live in hostility to his children. The willingness to face rejection and accept ridicule was part of the calling of his disciples. For most of our history, evangelicals, whatever our faults, trembled before eternity. We understood the gravity of such matters, deciding to follow Jesus, with "no turning back, no turning back," and we reckoned with the intensity that all this decision required.

There was also a time, and one not so long ago, when evangelical Christians regarded their marginal place in society as a mark of their faithfulness to Christ. Conformity and compromise were the great temptations, but the courage to stand true to our convictions was our great virtue, at least it was the devotion to which we aspired. We would have refused to cast aside the faith before the watching world. In Bible studies and prayer groups, we spoke of the martyrs as exemplars for our time and our witness. We told stories of men, women, and children who accepted persecution and death as the cost of their commitment. A parade of souls burning with the fire of God marched through the sermons and testimonials of the evangelical churches. "You are surrendering your lives to Christ," Billy Graham would say at the altar call. The words of the hymn, "Just as I am," bespoke the urgency of our condition. The heart's longings could be fulfilled only in Jesus, and in accepting the gift of salvation our lives would be lived as parables of gratitude.

More recently, the story of Cassie Bernall, one of the students murdered in the Columbine High School massacre in 1999, captivated the conservative churches in its attention to the weight of a single declaration of assent. "They asked her if she believed in God, and when she said 'yes' they shot her," a classmate recalled.[22] The evangelical bard, Michael W. Smith, wrote a ballad in her honor, "This Is Your Time," and a moving one indeed. Smith sang, "Faced with the choice to deny God and live, for her there was one choice to make." Cassie's "Yes" challenged the evangelical youth of the nation to boldly consider the prospect of accepting death for the sake of Christ, even in their own schools.

Those days are gone. And who can blame us? With all the networking and fundraising, handshaking and teleconferencing, there is no time for the fiery furnace. Instead we have decided to keep the fluorescent lights humming until the world has been made our home, and until every Bible-believing child, man, and woman has been accommodated, affirmed, and relieved finally of the anxieties of living in truth. An evangelical subculture that once venerated single-mindedness and passion has flown the ghetto for sure. The Jesus freaks became the political elites, and their convictions were sold on the market (or sometimes leased) to the highest bidder. Equipped with a savvier faith, access to political power became a far more thrilling accomplishment than standing up for Jesus in defiance of the assault weapons and the antichrists. The martyrs of the Christian tradition may have accepted death for the sake of the gospel and renounced vengeance against their oppressors, but now we serve a God who is "pro-war." No one talks about Cassie Bernall anymore.

But if Christians cannot confess Jesus as Lord of our lives, even, or especially when, we are faced with mockery or persecution, if we cannot present our bodies as a living sacrifice, "holy and acceptable to God," as Saint Paul writes, even, or especially when, we find ourselves assaulted by the dark powers and dominions of the world, if we cannot stand up for Jesus and confess with clarity that Christ is Lord over all creation—even over our violent world—then we have failed to live into the fullness of our salvation. In God's economy, it is not our prerogative to split the difference between devotion to partisan loyalties and discipleship to Jesus, or to demur on the authority of the latter in favor of the personal benefits of the former. Baptized in the name of the Father, Son, and Holy Spirit, we are born again, and as people who have been born again, we are brought into a new order. We are given new citizenship. We *are* a new creation.

Christians in the United States must resist the temptation to make the Christian faith relevant to our cultural needs. Jesus calls each of us, in our brokenness and rebellion, to take up our cross and follow him. Following Jesus brings with it certain and inevitable inconvenience not unlike that of living as a stranger in a strange land. Following Jesus means setting one's sights on the truth of God "at a time when all concepts are being confused, distorted and turned upside-down."[23]

Chapter Two

WHO IS THE GOD WE WORSHIP?

W HO WORSHIPS HERE?" Martin Luther King Jr. once asked
of the Protestant church in the South. "Who is their
God?"

We might ask a similar question. Who is the God white evangelicals worship in these late days, the deity fashioned in our
sermons, books, conferences, and campaigns? Does this God re-
semble the holy and righteous God of the Hebrew and Christian
Bible, the one who cautioned Moses, "Come no closer!" (Exod.
3:5), who demanded of Israel, "Thou shalt have no other gods
before me" (20:3), the "devouring fire" (24:17), the cloud cover-
ing the tent of the congregation, the one whom Saint Paul named
as the source of all wisdom, "the mystery that has been hidden
throughout the ages and generations but has now been revealed
to his saints" (Col. 1:26)? Or is the God we trust that of domesticated transcendence, the sound of middle-class family values
spoken in a shrill voice? Have we grown accustomed to hearing
the word intoned as a defense of our cultural preferences, rather

than as a summons to a new creation and new identity? "Come unto me, all ye that labour and are heavy laden, and I will give you rest," Jesus said (Matt. 11:28 KJV). I fear the faith has been stripped of its resplendent and demanding strangeness. John the Baptist, in the sixteenth-century painting by Matthias Grünewald, points ruefully toward the dying Savior, toward a greater and perfect holiness, but the American churches have blurred the lines of that essential difference. Who is our God?

"So for anyone who is in Christ," Saint Paul wrote to the church in Corinth, "there is a new creation." In this seaport town in Greece, members in the Christian community had forged a religious identification with influential political leaders rather than with Christ. In answer to their mistaken loyalty, Paul explained that in Christ, "the old order is gone and a new being is there to see" (2 Cor. 5:16–17 NJB).

Our president has said that when he speaks the words of the Lord's Prayer, "Thy will be done," he likes to add the phrase, "through me."[1] The president may have intended the remark as a straightforward expression of divine guidance, the sort familiar among evangelical Christians, the hope that his life would be an instrument of Providence. I surely hope that was his intention. But I also cannot help thinking that the added petition, "through me" registers more of a sense of entitlement than a petition. It's a lot for one man to ask for. I hear in the remark a clue to what has troubled me in recent years about the state of Christianity in America. We have come to regard ourselves as an indispensable part of the sovereign will of God. The "through me" hints at a messianic impulse, the all-about-*me* piety of the American dispensation. God could not possibly accomplish his will without our ingenuity and verve.

This is not the response of a grateful heart to the good news; it is rather what you might expect of a superhero coming to the rescue of a friend in need. "I couldn't have done it without you," the Almighty sighs with relief.

I RECENTLY TOOK A FEW DAYS to reread the war sermons delivered by influential evangelical ministers during the lead-up to the Iraq war. That period, from the fall of 2002 through the spring of 2003, will long be remembered as a sad chapter in the history of the Christian church. During those months, many of the most respected voices in American evangelical circles blessed the president's war plans, even when doing so often required them to recast, if not disregard or willfully misinterpret, Christian moral doctrine. Some ministers tried to square the American invasion with Christian "just war" theory, despite the fact that such efforts could never fulfill the criterion that force must be used only as a last resort. Others tried to link Saddam Hussein with wicked King Nebuchadnezzar of biblical fame, but these arguments depended on esoteric interpretations of Ezekiel and 2 Kings and could not easily be translated into the kinds of catchy phrases that are projected onto video screens in the evangelical worship centers. One heard no concern in the sermons for the global mission of the evangelical church or the integrity of Christian truth claims. And surprisingly (or maybe not), Jesus made only an occasional appearance, and then more as an aggravation to our political hopes than as the Lord of our faith. The Sermon on the Mount comes off looking like a profound nuisance, and was redacted and demythologized with a skill that would please any liberal biblical scholar. Nearly 80 percent of all white evangelical Christians in the United States supported the president's decision before the attack and an astonishing 87 percent in April of 2003.

Franklin Graham, whom I have already mentioned, the son of Billy Graham and heir ascendant to the evangelistic empire, claimed that our military forces in Iraq were preparing the way for the conversion of the Muslim world. Franklin Graham made this remark with the complete confidence that he was faithfully representing God in the public square.[2] Yet I am hard pressed to imagine a more chilling example of the messianic ego unleashed on the world stage. As if working from a slate of evangelical talking points, other leaders echoed the younger Graham's sentiment by claiming that the American invasion of Iraq would create exciting new prospects for Christian missions to Muslims. "American foreign policy and military might have opened an opportunity for the Gospel in the land of Abraham, Isaac, and Jacob," an article claimed in the publication, *Baptist Press*.[3] "God is moving here, and Southern Baptists are responding." Marvin Olasky, the editor of the conservative Christian magazine *World* and a former presidential consultant on faith-based issues, claimed that the war "will lead to liberation that will last, with Iraqis free to discuss both politics and the claims of Christ."[4] Similarly, when Jack Graham (no relation to Billy and Franklin), the president of the Southern Baptist convention, said at the conclusion of his enthusiastic defense of the invasion of Iraq, that "in these urgent days we will seize the opportunity to advance the Kingdom of God," he encouraged the perception that the church and the military were an interconnected part of the enormous providential campaign in the Middle East.[5]

And it didn't stop there. Paul Crouch, the glitzy founder of the

Trinity Broadcasting Network, blitzed the airwaves in an attempt to raise money for Iraqi churches—specifically, he said, for purchasing a satellite dish for every congregation in the invaded nation. "We are on our way with the true gospel of Jesus Christ," Crouch exclaimed.[6] The "brave military men and women" and the "mighty hand of God" are working in tandem to "penetrate" the Arab world with the gospel (and expand the global market for satellite dishes!).[7] Tim Lahaye, the author of the best-selling *Left Behind* series, spoke of Iraq as "a focal point of end-time events," whose special role in the earth's final days would become clear after invasion, conquest, and reconstruction. Iraq will emerge as a "sort of Switzerland for the world," Lahaye claimed. Numerous evangelical preachers around the United States made dramatic reference to "God's mysterious working in the world," as though the invading American army was being sent in preparation for the spiritual transformations that would follow.

But no one led the charge with greater fervor than Charles Stanley, pastor of the First Baptist Church of Atlanta, whose weekly sermons are seen by millions of television viewers. "We should offer to serve the war effort in any way possible," said Stanley, a former president of the Southern Baptist Convention. "God battles with people who oppose him, who fight against him and his followers." It would be "a violation of the Word of God to refuse to defend your country if ordered," Stanley said, citing the verse in the thirteenth chapter of Romans: "Let every soul be subject unto the higher powers. For there is no power but of God; the powers that be are ordained of God" (13:1 ASV). All the while, he ignored the equally confounding instruction in the twelfth chapter: "Bless your persecutors; never curse them, bless them" (12:14 NJB). Stanley claimed that "God favors war for divine purposes and sometimes uses it to accomplish His will"; the invasion of Iraq should thereby be accepted as part of God's sovereign and mysterious plan for the world.

The problem with this sermon, which was echoed in many of the other war homilies, is that it is, in short, a travesty of the gospel. Time and again, Stanley retreats from the Christian affirmation of Jesus Christ as the standard by which all faith and practice is judged, the church's one foundation. The sermon's tone of supreme self-confidence is horrifying. There is no anguish, no dark night of struggle, no wrestling with Scripture, as Stanley blithely ignores the enormous risks the church takes when it tells its children that to kill is not to murder. There is not a hint of apprehension, or words of caution, about the certain violence inflicted on civilians. There is no sense in which the believer must evaluate all moral decisions on the basis of the life and teachings of Jesus Christ, whose saving grace constitutes, to repeat, the final and absolute criterion of Christian faith and practice. One finds instead a demurral on the authority of Jesus Christ, a breathtaking shrug of indifference towards the world-changing, soul-saving ministry of the one who said, "I give you a new commandment, that you love one another. Just as I have loved you, you also should love one another" (John 13:34).

For ministers like Charles Stanley, the conclusion drawn is that, in the final analysis, the teachings of Jesus are irrelevant for Christian existence in the modern world. Jesus cannot be taken seriously by believers struggling to counter the forces of terrorism. Jesus' life, teachings, and saving love, his "philosophy", do not represent a new order created by God in time and history. They do not announce the coming of the kingdom of God. Although he steered clear of military service himself, Stanley speaks of war as a "positive."

I am not suggesting that Jesus' ethical teachings are unambiguous, or that there is no warrant in the Christian tradition for coercive action against unjust and dehumanizing forces. The gospel narratives are filled with moral complexity. But Jesus' teachings must intrude upon our confidences and cause aggravation to our well-laid plans. Jesus constantly surprises, confounds, and contests worldly powers, unlike such war preachers as Charles Stanley, whose defense of the American invasion of Iraq is entirely free of fear and trembling. The war preachers offered reassuring words to their flag-flying congregations, but they did so by demurring on the proclamation of Jesus Christ as Lord of the one church. Jesus may have suffered the humiliation and anguish of Golgotha's unspeakable horrors, making himself a sacrifice for the sins of the world, but esoteric interpretations of Ezekiel and of 2 Kings and high-camp nonsense about God's mysterious working in Iraq were the preferred themes when it came to the church's response to preemptive war. And this meant that in those rare instances in which the name of Jesus is invoked by the patriot preachers, it was usually done so obligingly, with the enthusiasm of a man nodding slightly in the direction of an unwanted guest.

"You may think, 'Well, how do we reconcile [war] with what Jesus said about loving our enemies and turning the other cheek?'" Stanley asked (Luke 6:27–30). "But: In that passage, Jesus was speaking to us as individuals." With one swat of the hand, Stanley put to rest the church's ancient wisdom of Jesus as the inauguration of the new order of God. The biblical scholar Richard

Hays wrote that "when we read the New Testament material on violence through the focal lens of community, we recognize that the church as a whole is called to live the way of discipleship and to exemplify the love of enemies."[8] Charles Stanley interprets the New Testament material on violence through the focal lens of American foreign policy and creates a new American Christ along the way. If Jesus is only speaking to us as individuals, everything is then negotiable.

Such consequential demurrals come with a cost. Karl Barth once observed of the German church in the early twentieth century that theologically the ship was without a rudder.[9] When I read the war sermons again, or listen to them on CD, which is a very depressing exercise, I detect more than a hint of annoyance with the gospel of Jesus Christ. I sense the rustling of feet in swift flight to safer ground. A reference to Jesus is almost always followed by a flurry of redacting, contextualizing, and demythologizing, interpretive practices commonly associated with liberal Protestant scholarship. The hard edge of the gospel recedes into the distance as a set of principles inspiring motivation and purpose takes its place. The teachings of Jesus have little bearing on political existence in the modern world. No doubt, the patriot preachers are in good company in their suspicion of the literal meaning of Jesus' words, but as evangelical Christians, they should not be so eager to indulge their suspicion.

"Our job is to reclaim America for Christ, whatever the cost," said James D. Kennedy, the president of Coral Ridge Ministries and minister of the Coral Ridge Presbyterian Church in Fort Lauderdale, Florida. "As the vice regents of God, we are to exercise godly dominion and influence . . . over every aspect and institution of human society."[10]

The war preachers have seen the face of God and discerned the secrets of the divine mind. They have been called to a high and holy calling, and as Kennedy said, "no power on earth can stop us."[11] Still, when I reread the sermons, what surprised me more than anything was discovering how much their single common theme appears to be this: Our president is a real brother in Christ, and since he has discerned that God's will for our nation is to wage war against Iraq, we must gloriously comply.

KARL BARTH'S OBSERVATION can be found in his essay "Evangelical Theology in the Nineteenth Century." Every Christian in the United States should purchase a copy of his book *The Humanity of God*, and read (and then reread) the essay that forms the first chapter of the book. Over the years, I have had many students tell me that the piece changed their way of thinking about the church's witness in the world.

In his essay, Barth recalled "a certain black day" in August 1914, when ninety-three German theologians and writers proclaimed their support of the war policy of Wilhelm II. On that day it became suddenly clear to Barth that he could no longer stand in the company of nineteenth-century Protestant liberal theologians. The religious scholars and writers had come to confuse the will of the nation with the will of God: Christian values and the Christian religion had gained preeminence over the Christian proclamation. The complicity with the war effort signaled to Barth that the religious elites of the German nation had given too much away to culture and politics. To be sure, they exhibited a robust engagement with the world, and this was a welcome change from self-imposed isolation and crusty dogmatism; nevertheless, their engagement with the world became an end in itself, and little attention was given to the uniqueness of the message and proclamation.[12] Outside winds brought not only fresh air into the Christian community but also "notoriously foul air," and as a result, fatal errors blew in, were accepted, and found a home in the church.[13] The Christian gospel was "changed into a statement," a principle for purposeful living, and "the God was lost sight of who in His sovereignty confronts man, calling him to account, and dealing with him as Lord." This loss further blurred the church's sight "horizontally," and the believer was in turn condemned to "uncritical and irresponsible subservience to the patterns, forces, and movements of human history and civilization."[14] In the end, the Christian faith became little more than an accoutrement of culture, a catalyst to the ambitions of an ambitious nation.

I think of Barth's "black day" when I revisit our own sad recent history. I am not sure that evangelicalism in the United States can survive its indulgence in "the arts of equivocation and pretense," and its contemptuous disregard of the global, ecumenical church.[15] But even if the conservative churches continue to grow and prosper, even if they continue to produce ever more effective innovations in worship and even more relevant, edgy, Bono-citing pastors, the air has grown foul, and our words no longer ring with authenticity. It might be better now to all be known simply as people who ask for forgiveness and in turn forgive others.

In the bible, we do not find God going in search of heroes and saints, of vice-regents and holy men, who will captivate the world with their charisma and verve. "Where is the one who is wise? Where is the scribe? Where is the debater of this age?" writes

Saint Paul. "Has not God made foolish the wisdom of the world?" (1 Cor. 1:20). God calls the unlikeliest of men and women, outcasts and misfits, reprobates and malcontents to live in grace. My minister in Virginia once made the point that when we look at the stories of the Bible's main characters, at King David, or the Samaritan woman at the well, or Saint Peter, we find God seeking out the company of sinners rather than those who presume themselves to be righteous and pure. In particular, in these stories we meet adulterers, adulteresses, and traitors who confess their brokenness and fallibility and then leave the old ordeal behind, trusting in God's promises to bless.[16]

James Kennedy's great self-commission echoes, in my view, the dangerous American presumption that God needs a special nation to unilaterally realize his purposes in the world. Now is a good time to remind ourselves of the basic Christian fact that God would be in every way God without America, and that God's relation to the world is based not on God's need of the world but on the overabundance of his love—on the ecstatic love of the Trinity, as the Christian tradition has often affirmed—and that only God is God. The good news is that though God is fully God *just being God*, nonetheless, God invites all humanity, in our sinfulness and rebellion, to join him in common history and to partake of his love in the community of Christ. The *Great Catechism* of the ancient church, one the earliest and most eloquent formulations of orthodox Christian belief, asserts: "If the entire world was created by [God's reason and wisdom], then certainly was man also thus created; yet not in view of any necessity, but from super-abounding love, that there might exist a being who should participate in the Divine perfections."[17]

Thomas Aquinas, one of the pillars of the Christian religion, regarded the basic Christian fact as the foundational conviction of orthodox belief. God would be perfectly God had he not created the world. God did not need the world in order to be God; God did not need the world so that he might (as the philosopher Hegel would later claim) recognize his divinity in creation and thereby achieve a greater self-realization. God did not need the world in order to reach a deeper integration with his divine nature. Aquinas believed that the idea of necessity would in turn place limits on God, which could easily be turned into a claim. Still, to say that God was no less God before he created the world, no less perfect, and no less good, merciful, and gracious, is not to say that God is indifferent to the world or uninvolved with people. The "Christian distinction," as the Catholic philosopher Robert Sokolowski has named it, attributes to God perfection beyond necessity. "[The] world is not diminished in its own excellence," Professor Sokolowski says, "rather the world is now understood as not having had to be. If it did not have to be, it is there out of choice. And if the choice was not motivated by any need of completion in the one who let it be, and not motivated by the need for 'there' to be more perfection and greatness, then the world is there through an incomparable generosity."[18] Therefore, the world exists "simply for the glory of God." In this way, the glory of God is seen not only in the exquisite variety of the world but "in the very existence of the world and everything in it."[19]

This means that God created the universe in its variety and detail out of his ecstatic and creative love. The world exists as an expression of an "incomparable generosity": *God the Trinity*, Father, Son, and Holy Spirit, living in perfect unity, *reaching out in love to create the world*.[20] What wonderful news this is: God's unconditional invitation to join him in shared history, the one pure gift in a world of "unjust ugliness," the free and gratuitous expression of God's everlasting love.[21] Christians worship a God whose love surprises and arrests, as a light springing out of darkness.

We must then reckon with the truth of the basic axiom of orthodox Christianity and allow ourselves to be chastened by its unsettling truth: God does not need America in order to be God. God thus requires all nations to fulfill his moral purposes.

P̲AT ROBERTSON IS ANOTHER of the evangelical elites who has seen God face-to-face. God has revealed deep secrets to Robertson, knowledge of things nowhere found in Scripture or in tradition. For example, God told Robertson that feminism leads women to "kill their children" as well as to "practice witchcraft, destroy capitalism and become lesbians."[22] God told him that the city of Orlando, Florida, would be cursed with a hurricane if Disney World hosted a Gay Pride Day at the family-friendly theme park.[23] God told Robertson (and his Virginia cohort Falwell) that the terrorist attacks of September 11, 2001, came as punishment on a nation that had climbed into bed with "the pagans, and the abortionists, and the feminists, and the gays and the lesbians."[24]

Pat Robertson's pronouncements have been become as predictable as they are offensive. After his much ballyhooed recommendation that CIA operatives assassinate President Hugo Chavez of Venezuela, the *Times* called him "a garden-variety crackpot."[25] Not many other crackpots get as much attention in lead editorials on the op-ed page of the major dailies. Eugene Robertson wrote in the *Washington Post*, "I thought the bumpersticker slogan was 'Jesus Is My Co-Pilot,' not 'Jesus Is My Hit Man.'"[26]

On *The Larry King Show*, the evangelical pastor Ted Haggard, who once served as president of the thirty-million strong National Association of Evangelicals, came to the defense of Robertson after his call for the assassination of President Hugo Chavez. Pat's *700 Club* "actually has two different programs with separate agendas," Haggard explained. One program features Robertson going about the business of "Christian exhortation," preaching, teaching, and praying with his various prayer partners. In the other, Robertson appears in the role of political pundit. Haggard explained grimly that we should evaluate his political views in the context of the pundit persona.

When comedian Jon Stewart replayed Haggard's explanation on Comedy Central's *Daily Show*—with a homely portrait of Jesus flashing on the screen—Stewart offered his own theological analysis of Robertson's split identity. "I mean . . . have you ever tried to live your life by the things this [Jesus] said? I mean after an hour you need some 'Me' time." (We would soon learn that Pastor Ted was no stranger to "me time." In November of 2006, he was caught consorting with a male prostitute and purchasing illegal drugs.)

The secular media have gone to great lengths to convince Americans that Robertson's outbursts should not be taken seriously. The *Washington Post* noted Robertson's "long history of pious bloviations"; his opinions were "witless," "ill-advised," "moronic," "callow," and "downright loopy." Recently, evangelicals have joined the chorus of critics. In criticism of Robertson's comments on Chavez, Al Mohler, the dean of the fundamentalist Southern Baptist Theological Seminary, said, "He has brought embarrassment upon us all. With so much at stake, Pat Robertson bears responsibility to retract, rethink, repent, and restate his position on this issue." Responding to Robertson's claim that God had personally offered him a guarantee of Bush's reelection, conservative Christian columnist Cal Thomas said, "This is subjective religion. If one 'feels,' it's 'real.' Religious feelings supplant objective truth and make the individual a high priest unto himself, above mere mortals who apparently are not on the 'A' access-to-God list." "Jesus called for nothing like this, and Pat Robertson sounded more like one of the radical imams," the distinguished evangelical writer Os Guinness remarked on ABC's *World News Tonight*.

Still, I think Pat Robertson's split personality—the one praying for healing and the other advising a hit job—helps us get to the bottom of the prevailing evangelical confusion. His strange career should not be so quickly dismissed as rantings from the lunatic fringe. In fact, the case of Pat Robertson perfectly illustrates the confused loyalties of contemporary evangelicals. We have not figured out whether it is our mission to proclaim salvation to the nations, to call men and women to join the "God Movement" (in the words of the old Southern Baptist progressive Clarence Jordan), or to impose our own designs on the nations, presuming that our ambitions fit neatly into God's will. Robertson has become unbearable to most evangelicals because he exposes the utter confusion about who we are and what we should be doing. We dare not dismiss him as "a garden-variety crackpot with friends in high places."[2] He is us.

I THINK THIS WAR HAS MADE us a meaner nation. The signs are everywhere: on television and radio shows, in the airports and on the highways, in the aggressive habits of powerful institutions.

Recently a Dodge Caravan sped passed me on the interstate with a red and black bumper sticker saying; "God bless America— and to Hell with Our Enemies." The nation's highways and roads of the nation have become death zones, where size and speed determine the rules and more than 55,000 people are killed each year. Gigantic trucks furiously crisscross the country threatening oblivion to anyone in their way. The demonic gun industry, desperately in search of new customers, solicits children and teenagers in a variety of cunning forms. Introduced to the exciting possibilities of destroying human life in the simulated murder stations in their own living rooms, the video game industry comprises a large and emerging market and domesticates the horror of mass death. In an industry trade magazine, an advertisement for a gun shop in the Midwest features a blond-haired girl smiling in front of a wall of semi-automatic weapons. The little girl is holding a gun and is wearing a two-piece swim suit; but even more shocking is that men and women calling themselves American (and Christian) patriots organize tirelessly in support of this pornography of violence.

Our beloved Billy Graham's retirement leaves us with a generation of Christians raised on *Left Behind* novels, church-growth consultations, talk radio, and seminary trainings bereft of critical thought. On the eve of the American invasion of Iraq, Rush Limbaugh argued daily that the welfare of Iraqi civilians should be of little concern to our nation as it makes plans for war. Worrying about innocent Iraqi life was a distraction we needed to get over. Rush ruled indeed: Conservative Christians and Rush walked hand-in-hand to the brink of heresy. More influential than Pope John Paul II and the new Pope Benedict, and more

influential than the leaders of every denomination (except the
Southern Baptist Convention) and the entire global Christian
community, Rush's views prevailed when it came to buttressing
public opinion on Iraq. Still, one might even wonder whether Mr.
Limbaugh himself (in the late hours when his mind turns darkly)
is unsettled by the popularity of his anti-Christian life-boat
ethics among listeners who call themselves followers of Jesus.[28]
On the other hand, this is a pundit who has ridiculed the Christian Peacemaker Teams and their global reconciliation work, dismissed them as people "practicing a bunch of irresponsible,
idiotic theory," and who once said of the arrest and torture of
Christian Peacemakers in Iraq, "Folks, there's a part of me that
likes this."

So here we are: instead of Billy Graham's invitation to the
altar of forgiveness, the words of our ditto-headed disciples are
launched against decency and compassion like crusading missiles.
We do not hear the gentle summons of "Just as I Am" from the
vice-regents and the born-again demagogues—or from Jesus-
despisers like Rush Limbaugh. We hear base and sinful thoughts
disguised as moral values.

Let us not forget too that many of the conservative evangelicals
who campaigned loudly for the nation's revenge of September 11
by invading Iraq believe wholeheartedly in a God who will someday gather up these same men, women, and children—every last
one who perished on that horrible Tuesday morning—and submit
them to his Last Judgment, and those he finds to be unfit for
heaven will be cast into an eternity of flames. And this same God
will watch these lost souls suffer, once again, in final torment and
terror, in an everlasting hell of his own design, in a lake of fire

large enough for every non-Christian man, woman, and child who
ever lived, however good, well-meaning, or trustworthy. The same
Christians who believe in this final divine judgment which condemns not only Anne Frank and Mahatma Gandhi but most
people, living or dead, look forward to that day of wrath and pray
for its swift arrival with the certainty that they shall be spared
God's wrath, and that cruel certainty is the presupposition that
shapes all their judgments and beliefs about the nation and the
world. That certainty defines their basic understanding the human condition.

SUCH SENTIMENTS AS THESE ABOVE are a far cry from those of the
1974 Lausanne Covenant, whose significance in the evangelical
movement I claimed earlier should not be understated and whose
generous internationalism serves to remind us of how far we have
strayed from the confession of the church's global unity in
Christ. The drafters of the Lausanne Covenant, working under
the leadership of John Stott, had affirmed the global character of
the church of Jesus Christ and their belief that "the church is the
community of God's people rather than an institution, and must
not be identified with any particular culture, social or political
system, or human ideology." The gospel is a "precious treasure"
and "God's news for the whole world," the Covenant noted.[29]

In an op-ed piece in the *New York Times*, which appeared in
the spring of 2004, the conservative writer David Brooks noted
that if evangelicals were able to elect a pope, it would most likely
be Stott, the author of more than forty books on evangelical theology and Christian devotion and rector emeritus at All Soul's,
Langham Place, London. But unlike the Pope John Paul II who

said that invading Iraq would violate Catholic moral teaching and threaten "the fate of humanity," or even Pope Benedict XVI, who said there were "not sufficient reasons to unleash a war against Iraq," Stott did not speak publicly on the Iraq issue in the months preceding war. In an interview for this book, however, Dr. Stott shared with me his abiding concerns.

"Privately, in the days preceding the invasion, I had hoped that no action would be taken without UN authorization," he said. "I believed then and now that the American and British governments erred in proceeding without UN approval."

The Reverend Dr. Stott referred me to "War and Rumours of War," a chapter in his 1999 book, *New Issues Facing Christians Today*, as the best account of his current position. In that essay he wrote that the Christian community's primary mission must be "to hunger for righteousness, to pursue peace, to forbear revenge, to love enemies, in other words, to be marked by the cross."

What will it take for American evangelicals to recognize our mistaken loyalty? We have increasingly isolated ourselves from the shared faith of the global church, and there is no denying that our Faustian bargain for access and power has undermined the credibility of our moral and evangelistic witness in the world. The Hebrew prophets might call us to repentance, but repentance is a difficult demand for a people convinced of their righteousness.

Chapter Three
THE PIETY OF COSMIC ENTITLEMENT

I REGRET HAVING TO SPEAK OF THE PRESIDENT'S FAITH. I stand convicted no less than any other person by Jesus' words to the Pharisees, "Why beholdest thou the mote that is in thy brother's eye, but considerest not the beam that is in thine own eye?" (Matt. 7:3 KJV). I pray for the president each Sunday as I read with my fellow parishioners from the Book of Common Prayer. I pray for George our president, Richard our vice president, and other political leaders in our nation and state, including Timothy the Virginia governor. Nevertheless, as a believer and a theologian who cares deeply about the integrity of Christian conviction in our time, I cannot exempt the vivid displays of the president's faith from our theological analysis of American evangelicalism.

Discussions of the piety of George W. Bush have often focused on the sincerity of his convictions. Critics charge that his faith is narcissistic, opportunistic, or politically calculated. Some church-traditionalists have worried that his faith lacks accountability to the authority and disciplines of the Christian community.

The president's indifference to the stated opposition of nearly every Christian denomination to the American invasion of Iraq, including his own United Methodist Church, is regarded as a symptom of baby-boomer spirituality, which cavalierly picks and chooses its deity and style of worship according to subjective measures of comfort, conviction, and commitment. The journalist Amy Sullivan has written that the president's preference for worship is for the military chapel at Camp David, staffed by Marine chaplains, and an Episcopal church in Washington, where he occasionally makes an appearance.[1]

I agree that sporadic church attendance for the most aggressively evangelical president in history is perplexing. Still, however important these matters might be, my main concern is not to nitpick over church attendance or to question the sincerity of the president's belief. Rather, my concern is to explore how it has come to be that George W. Bush—whose fawning religiosity runs counter to orthodox Christianity in many significant ways—has been wholeheartedly claimed by conservative believers as "the real deal in terms of his walk with Christ."[2] What exactly is it about the faith of this president that has enabled him to attract unprecedented numbers of evangelicals and to exemplify to these evangelicals true religiosity? What did George W. Bush do and say to gain near unanimous approval among white evangelicals, to be regarded as a true Bible-believing Christian? Political and policy factors have no doubt played a role in his influence and popularity, but what are the theological sources of the churches' widespread excitement?

SOME INFLUENTIAL PUBLIC INTELLECTUALS have speculated that the president's theological worldview is shaped by the apocalyptic and premillennialist views of a certain hard-edged variety of Christian fundamentalism, and they have asked whether the religious advisors who serve him adhere to these grim doctrines. The premillennialist Christian believes that Jesus will return again to earth in the second coming, and that he will rapture his church after momentous events involving the nation of Israel have been fulfilled.[3] The prospect that large portions of the GOP have surrendered to an end-times theology is worrisome in the extreme.

But I do not think worries about an apocalyptic president are justifiable. On this point, I agree with the literary critic and Wheaton College professor Alan Jacobs, who wrote in the *Boston Globe* that "the likelihood that [Bush's] thinking and his policies are shaped by a single, coherent, radical ideology is virtually nil."[4] There might be evangelicals in the president's inner circle who believe the last days are upon us, though that seems unlikely. If the president's inner advisors have lost any sleep over the rapture, it's probably because they burned the midnight oil searching *Left Behind* novels for clues to winning the evangelical vote. What perplexes me instead are the false notes in the president's efforts to pitch himself (and to allow himself to be hailed) as America's Great Man of God.

Billy Graham once told the journalist and biographer Marshall Frady that his shock was so great upon hearing President Nixon's White House tapes, peppered as they were with profanities and racial epithets for his Democratic opponents, that he wept, felt nauseated, and then vomited for hours. Having been played for a fool by the Nixon administration, Graham resolved to distance himself from political endorsements of any kind. "I never dreamed . . . I just could never conceive . . . it was all something totally foreign . . . I never saw that side," Graham stuttered.[5] The sullen

Quaker president had gone to near comical lengths to ingratiate himself to evangelicals, even claiming in Graham's magazine, *Decision*, that he, Richard Milhous Nixon, had walked the aisle and accepted Christ as his personal Lord and Savior in one of the crusade services. Graham's resolution to steer clear of partisan loyalties was inspired not only by the shocking content of the tapes—the barrage of the president's "f-words" and desk-clearing temper tantrums—but also by his belief that he had been deliberately used by the White House; consequently Graham acknowledged his own capacity for self-deception and hankering for praise along with a certain willfulness to broker religious capital for political access. "Becoming involved in strictly political issues or partisan politics inevitably dilutes the evangelist's impact and compromises his message," Graham explained in his autobiography. "An evangelist is called to do one thing, and one thing only: to proclaim the Gospel."[6]

Of course, this is not the end of the story. Graham has continued to pray with presidents in politically intense moments of national-historical significance. The first President Bush summoned Graham to the White House for prayer on the eve of the 1991 Gulf War. The next evening, George H. W. Bush launched operation Desert Storm, and American military forces invaded Iraq in retaliation of its occupation of neighboring Kuwait. Prayer time with Graham gave legitimacy to Bush's decision, and the president's press secretary made sure the visit from Graham was noted far and wide. Graham may have seen his service to the president that night as straightforwardly pastoral, but the meeting helped create the impression that God's will had been discerned in the decision to launch Desert Storm. Naïve or willing accomplice, Graham had been used to cover the nation's military plans in the garment of Christian devotion. "We're down on our knees hoping these guys will crack," one military advisor said.[7]

THE SECOND PRESIDENT BUSH'S RELATIONSHIP to Graham, and to God, is a lot more complicated. Even the president's hagiographers stumble. David Aikman, author of *A Man of Faith: The Spiritual Journey of George W. Bush,* a glowing portrait of America's first "mere Christian" president, has noted the strange dislocation between Bush's numerous conversion experiences and his ostensible lack of interest in the intellectual and theological dimensions of Christianity.[8]

Much attention has been given to the dramatic born-again conversion story of George W. Bush, but the odd question of which conversion story muddies the water here as well. The president prefers the one featuring Billy Graham; nevertheless, as some journalists have noted, Bush's first born-again experience was not the frequently cited fireside chat and midnight seaside stroll in 1985 at Kennebunkport. This would come later. Bush's first conversion took place during his 1984 visit with the street evangelist Arthur Blessitt in the town of Midland, Texas.

Arthur Blessitt is nothing if not a great confounder of the world's wisdom. I met him in the summer of 1969, when I was traveling with my parents in California during the height of the Jesus Movement.[9] Blessitt had chained himself to a twelve-foot wooden cross and bolted the cross to a light pole on Sunset Boulevard in Hollywood. He had been evicted from the storefront street ministry called "His Place" and was fasting until authorities found his evangelistic work another home base. They soon did.

Some people called Blessitt the "psychedelic evangelist" because he used such phrases as "turning on to Jesus" and "eternal rush" to describe the emotional benefits of a personal relationship with Jesus. Blessitt claims to have carried his cross to every nation on earth and logged more than 37,000 miles on foot to share his faith in Jesus. His missionary sojourns earned him a spot in the Guinness Book of World's Records for world's longest walk. In the spring of 1984, Blessitt's endeavors carried him to the Texas heartland where he led a seven-day crusade. George W. Bush was in his late thirties at the time, working in the oil business. When he heard that the peripatetic preacher Blessitt was in town, he asked for a private meeting. "I want to talk to you about how to know Jesus Christ and how to follow him," Bush said.[10] Blessitt was impressed with the young businessman's "direct and sincere approach," and during their visit Blessitt asked Bush whether he had accepted Jesus Christ as his personal Lord and Savior.

"I'm not sure," Bush said.

Blessitt asked Bush whether he were confident that if he died at that moment, he would go to heaven.

"No," Bush answered.

Blessitt explained that a person becomes a Christian only by acknowledging his sins against God, praying for forgiveness, and accepting Jesus as the Lord of his life.

"Would you rather live with Jesus in your life or live without Him?" Blessitt asked.

"With Him," Bush said.

"Had you rather spend eternity with Jesus or without Him?" Blessitt asked.

"With Jesus," Bush said.

Blessitt then reached out and held the hand of the man who would become the nation's forty-third president. Blessitt led Bush in the sinner's prayer: "Dear God I believe in you and I need You in my life . . . Take control of my life . . . Make my home in Heaven and write my name in Your book in Heaven. I accept the Lord Jesus Christ as my Savior and desire to be a true believer in and follower of Jesus." Blessitt noted that Bush's "firm strong, [*sic*] but tender" grip tightened as the two men prayed together.

When the prayer was finished, Blessitt exclaimed, "There is rejoicing in Heaven now! You are saved! *There is joy in the presence of the angels of God over one sinner who repents.*"[11]

However, George W. Bush seemed singularly unmoved by the encounter. The biographer David Aikman notes that none of Bush's friends in Midland, Texas, observed any changes in his behavior in the wake of this born-again experience. Bush continued to socialize with friends and drink in excess.[12] It is not clear that he even spoke of the conversion to anyone at the time.

A year later, Bush had another born-again experience, the "life-changing" visit in 1985 with Billy Graham.[13] Although Graham has never mentioned this visit in his interviews or writings, Bush has made frequent reference to the Kennebunkport encounter in conversations, speeches, and writings. (Bush has never acknowledged saying the sinner's prayer with Arthur Blessitt, although Blessitt, who continues to walk the globe with his cross-on-wheels, has reported it in detail, as have Bush's most sympathetic biographers.[14]) Still, the way Bush talks about the transformative encounter, the intense fireside chats and soul-cleansing beach walks, is revealing; what captivated him most "was not so much

Graham's teaching" but the way the evangelist "made you feel loved," the way "he didn't make you feel guilty."[15] Bush's mother, Barbara, remembers the family visits with Graham as times when the children had a chance to ask questions about their spiritual lives. But the only question anyone recalls George W. Bush asking was whether some sins were worse than others. "Sin is sin," Graham replied.[16]

The *Christianity Today* writer Tony Carnes, in his article "A Presidential Hopeful's Progress: The Spiritual Journey of George W. Bush Starts in Hardscrabble West Texas," said that on one of their private walks, Graham and Bush discussed religious questions in detail. According to Carnes, Graham asked Bush, "Are you right with God?" and Bush responded, "No, but I want to be."[17] Nevertheless, in *A Charge to Keep*, Bush said he actually could not remember what he said to Graham, or what Graham said to him, on that life-changing weekend. "[We] walked and talked at Walker's Point, and I knew I was in the presence of a great man," Bush recalled. "[Billy Graham] was like a magnet; I felt drawn to seek something different. He didn't lecture or admonish; he shared warmth and concern."[18]

Despite the fuzzy memories of the conversation, Bush would later describe the meeting as the most significant moment in his spiritual pilgrimage. "It was the beginning of a new walk where I would recommit my heart to Jesus Christ."[19] The president says he began reading his Bible daily and felt freer about being a man of faith. "Scripture took on greater meaning, and I gained confidence and understanding in my faith."[20] David Aikman described the president's encounter with Graham as "the absolutely decisive event" in his journey of becoming a "follower of

Christ." But there are too many decisive life-changing moments, and there is too little learned. And through it all, Bush kept drinking abusively.

ONE YEAR LATER, on the eve of his fortieth birthday, Bush appeared to be coming unhinged. His closest friends were concerned, and rumors spread that Laura had issued an ultimatum. Bush's "continuing evening rounds of alcoholic conviviality," as Aikman refers to the binges, were wearing down his body and his mind. Reports of public drunkenness, temper tantrums, and bouts of profanity circulated in the liberal and conservative media.

On July 12, 1986, after a long night of partying at a birthday celebration in the mountains of Colorado, George W. Bush had another life-changing experience. The party had been held at the Broadmoor Hotel, the posh resort near Pikes Peak, and went until the early hours. Without divulging details, Don Evans, one of his drinking partners and a fellow born-again Christian, hinted that the festivities got of out of control. The next morning, the whole group was too hung over to visit the Air Force Academy Chapel, and Bush struggled to make it through his daily compensatory jog. He returned to the hotel and told Laura that he had decided to give up alcohol once and for all.

The decision was "one of the best things I have ever done," Bush said.[21] "Quitting drinking made me more focused and more disciplined." After the 2000 election, Bush told the speechwriter David Frum that "there is only one reason I am in the Oval Office and not in a bar: I found faith. I found God. I am here because of the power of prayer." In his biography, Aikman claimed that the Broadmoor experience brought Bush into a new life, "unencumbered by old, strong, alcohol-induced habits," where he could finally live boldly as a Christian.

But the Texas evangelist and Republican loyalist James Robison visited Bush in 1992, six years after the Colorado conversion, seven years after the Kennebunkport confessional with Billy Graham, eight years after the sinner's prayer with Arthur Blessitt, and two years before becoming governor of Texas, and Robison was struck by the man's immaturity. Bush seemed mostly "fun-seeking and sports-crazed," Robison said, even though Bush was now, presumably, clean and sober.[22]

Stretching further the credibility of the evangelical testimonial, a tradition that clusters around stories of brokenness, contrition, and new birth, and that stresses public confession and probing self-examination, Bush has never admitted to being an alcoholic.[23]

LET ME BE CLEAR ON ONE POINT. The president does not owe the American public a word about his private spiritual life, and, besides that, I think Christians in the United States should seriously consider casting their vote in the next election for the candidate who says the least about God. The problem is that telling half the story or leaving the job of his testimony to press secretaries and ghost writers—as Bush has often done—creates profound theological confusion. Taken at face value, the president's conversion narratives, considered as a whole, portray him as a serial converter. After the Broadmoor debacle, he says, "my life changed in many ways. An example is I quit drinking. I was a more dedicated, more focused person. Not to say I wasn't a dedicated person beforehand, but it was a life-changing moment."[24] The classic evangelical testimony, on the other hand, is distinguished by the unflinching and sometimes graphic honesty of the sinner in the hands of a righteous God.

To be sure, evangelical conversion narratives are also filled with stories of backsliding and failure, but no one is talking about backsliding and failure here. Bush's serial converting is in a league of its own. Moments of eternal clarity and supreme self-certainty followed by a divine summons to global power (with "only if that's God's will" added to reassure anyone left among the base who needed some shred of humility) announce the astonishingly good luck of having been summoned by God to a world-epochal mission. We might call that the piety of cosmic entitlement.

Although President Bush eagerly informed the nation during the 2000 Republican primary debates that Jesus Christ was his favorite philosopher, he wasn't interested in talking about the difference Jesus makes in the intellectual and moral shape of a life. What happens when the philosophy of Jesus Christ comes into conflict with decisions about war, poverty, wealth, and the like? It has always struck me as odd that evangelicals were so completely taken by Bush's remark, inclined as we are to speak of Jesus as the Son of God *rather than* as a philosopher or wise man. The Christian apologist C. S. Lewis's near canonical words in *Mere Christianity* echo in our ears when we hear references to Jesus as an exemplar of wisdom. "You must make your choice," said Lewis famously. "Either this man was, and is, the Son of God: or else a madman or something worse . . . But let us not come with any patronizing nonsense about His being a great human teacher. He has not left that open to us."[25]

I do not mean to be pedantic, but the very phrase "Jesus

Christ is the greatest philosopher because he changed my life" irritates on many levels. Is Jesus the greatest philosopher because he changed the president's life? Or is Jesus, and his philosophy, the greatest because Jesus speaks the truth? Because he is truth? If so, then the president would need to answer questions about how the philosophy of Jesus Christ obligates him to think differently about ideas and policies in all areas of life.

Bush's famous remark was completely lacking in theological substance; tactically, of course, it was dead on. The sight of the seven Republican candidates, getting beat to the draw by the straight-shooting Texas governor, scrambling awkwardly for another way to spin the same answer but falling short, was embarrassing in the extreme. Still, the real loser of the evening was not poor Orrin Hatch, who stumbled out his lame agreement with Bush, or Gary Bauer, who did more or less the same, but the Nazarene carpenter who proclaimed the coming of the kingdom of God. And in my view, the real winner was not George W. Bush but John McCain, who avoided the God-trap altogether and claimed Teddy Roosevelt as his greatest influence.

But on this question of Bush's evangelical mandate, I keep scratching my head over his not seeming to know when he became a Christian. If the president were a Catholic or a liberal Protestant, such a detail would not be so much of a problem, given their differing formulations of conversion. But the evangelical tradition differs markedly from liberal Protestantism and Catholicism in this regard, placing a high priority on the sinner's ability to recall the salvation moment with maximum detail and clarity. A vivid recollection of the moment of decision is one of the main themes of the "personal testimony." Astonishingly, when pressed on the matter by reporters, the president deferred to Karl

Rove and Karen Hughes, who in turn assumed the job of relating the details of their boss's spiritual journey. Rove and Hughes gave it their best shot, but the results were strained. "What I've always heard [President Bush] say is that he renewed his faith," Hughes said. "The Christian faith is the process of the Holy Spirit converting you, and you become more Christlike." "For the president, it was the wonderment of Graham's watching him," Rove explained. "Billy Graham was watching the interplay of [Bush] and his family, and he asked, 'Do you have the right relationship with God?'"[26]

Perhaps Aikman gets closest to the real motivation of Bush's serial conversions in his remark that through friendships with evangelical elites, "George W. learned invaluable lessons about what would later become the most important political base of his own run for the presidency."[27] Bush learned the subculture's idiom, the insider's talk (at least well enough), the buzz words, and the familiar intonations. On the threshold of unprecedented access to power, evangelicals were thrilled Bush even tried. "He knew their language," said Aikman.[28] He was the "real deal." But this brings me to a lingering suspicion about the story that I have not yet mentioned. I do not think the president is an evangelical, or, more precisely, I do not think he really considers himself one. It is not necessary to look into the man's heart to conclude that he is more comfortable with the default language of American civil religion, baby-boomer syncretism, and sporadic church attendance (and tailoring the services to his own tastes) than developing a worldview shaped by the Christian gospel (after he finishes). But this also means that he will someday have to seize upon other experiences than governing the American nation to keep alive his sense of divine calling or else face near unbearable despair.

George W. Bush is best described as a willing accomplice in the desperate evangelical search for the Godly Man in the Oval Office. He is willing because he likes the sentiment, the approvals and prayerful affirmations showered upon him by the support base. But he has not a single obvious intellectual investment in the truth claims or foundational beliefs of Christianity. His distinguishing feature is a shrugging indifference to complexity. Who needs the dark night of the soul when the world shines in perpetual noonday effulgence? With apologies to the conspiracy theorists who have speculated about a LaHaye-Cheney-Dobson axis of theological mischief, the content of Bush's faith comes straight from peppy worship centers in suburban/exurban tracts, from smiling preachers in sports arenas, from the thought-free Christian book chains where John Calvin and Martin Luther, even Carl F. H. Henry and J. Gresham Machen, have been replaced by Warren, Lucado, Dobson, and Colson—and where it is easier to find a copy of Bill Frist's speeches than the Nicene Creed or the Westminster Confession. It's all about God-and-me.

As for the president's claim (or actually Karl Rove's on his behalf) to read daily from Oswald Chambers's *My Utmost for His Highest*, I have my doubts. Identifying with this evangelical devotional classic no doubt elicits deep affinities with the subculture, but Chambers's severe wisdom discourages pride, emotional frivolity, careless speech, and every other self-aggrandizing quality of contemporary Washington godspeak.

Still, we should not be sanguine about the piety of cosmic entitlement and its global ramifications. In many respects, this piety may prove to be more menacing than the doomsday theology of the apocalyptic crowd. For the Christian president has boldly gone beyond the Reformation doctrines of *sola scriptura* and *sola fides* and embraced a distinctively American religiosity that empowers him with an immediate grasp of the divine will for the chosen nation. On a Texas Sunday morning, then Governor George W. Bush heard God say to him, "I want you to be President of the United States of America." By contrast, the Hebrew patriarch Moses, the archetypal leader in the Bible, protested the mantle of leadership when he was called by God. "Oh my Lord, please send someone else," Moses said.

All of this leads me to conclude that the president's piety is less indebted to Protestant evangelicalism than to certain forms of religious mysticism existing on the periphery of Christian orthodoxy. Look closely upon his demeanor when he invokes the name of God, for he appears at these moments as one who has seen God face to face. The president does not need church, tradition, or hierarchy; he has penetrated into the divine essence. He has gone where no man has gone before. He is an intimate of God, perfect in knowledge and wisdom, and he stutters as one who has passed through ecstasy. We are expected to accept his guidance without question, for he has joined a select company of mortals who behold the divine mystery and survived. He has become greater than Moses on the mount.

American evangelicals flock to Bush because they too want direct access to God: God without mediation, without the nuisance of tradition, without the global test. The ecumenical church is filled with critics and know-it-alls; the doctrines and creeds are complex and creaky; the canons of Christian thought, the theological tradition, are such a drag; there is no room in a righteous nation for fallible minds. The Reformation theologian John Calvin described the effects of Adam's disobedience as a disruption of our ability to know and to see and to interpret the world. But the evangelical elites have boldly cast aside the fall in pursuit of divine attributes of their very own. They are the vice-regents of God called to govern the nations.

The second-century theologian Irenaeus of Lyons described the redemptive death of Jesus Christ as the hidden center of all being, the sum of the world's known and unknown longings, which recapitulates the whole of estranged and broken creation to its original purpose. The incarnation revivifies the deep structures of the created order so that all creation and all its exquisite diversity are "gathered together, included and comprised" in Christ—the real history of the world is revealed in the story of Jesus. Irenaeus explained in his treatise *Against Heresies*, "[As] in super-celestial, spiritual and invisible things, the Word is Supreme, so also in things visible and corporeal He might possess the supremacy, and taking to Himself the preeminence, as well as constituting Himself Head of the Church, He might draw all things to Himself at the proper time."[29] Jesus Christ redeemed, reconstructed, and reconstituted the created order, which until the coming of God in the flesh had been subjected to final obliteration, estranged from its source, advancing in a slow but certain march into non-being. But the incarnation of God in Jesus Christ is the advent of perfect peace, which Christians believe to be the real meaning of life—life lived more abundantly.

These are sublime and ponderous notions, the story of the whole architecture of being crumbling beneath the weight of human rebellion yet redeemed now in the coming of the Messiah, and it is a conception that once grasped inspires the mind towards a joyful but sober apprehension of reality: Christ representing in word and truth the first Adam, rescuing in himself "all the dispersed peoples dating back to Adam, all tongues and the whole race of mankind, along with Adam himself," "recapitulating in Himself the long sequence of mankind."[30] And this means that now, in the time after the great event of the cross and resurrection, we see all things under a new light. Celebrating life with God, we accept the good news that Jesus has taken the place of our judgment, suffered on the cross for the disobedience of Adam, and born the punishment that we deserve, gathering up all humanity into the fellowship of the Father, Son, and Holy Spirit.

In a letter from Tegel prison, where he spent the final years of his life before being executed by the Gestapo in 1945, Dietrich Bonhoeffer recalled Irenaeus's idea as a "magnificent conception," "full of comfort." "Everything is taken up in Christ," Bonhoeffer said, "although it is transformed."[31] Irenaeus's account of the ontological rebirth of the world in Christ brings relief and consolation. We learn that the Christian's primary mission is to learn to be a participant in God's good and glorious creation. We are relieved of the burden to recreate the world in our own image and the exhausting task of seeking to orchestrate God's will; for it is Christ and Christ alone who "give[s the world] back to us" as a gift.[32]

What does this ancient Christian formulation have to do with evangelical behavior in the present time? I can imagine Irenaeus, in the company of the church fathers and mothers, the saints and the martyrs, and all the faithful stewards of Christian truth over our two-thousand-year history, looking upon the whole spectacle of American Christendom, with its grotesque shrinking of salvation's sweep to the narrow agendas of individuals and groups and its presumption to know God, and God's purposes apart from Scripture, church, and tradition, as something quite foreign to the historic faith of revealed Christianity, indeed as a theological

system they might even regard as heretical. "Heresy is a deliberate denial of revealed truth coupled with the acceptance of error" is the definition given in the *Evangelical Dictionary of
Theology*.[33] Unlike the apostate, who rejects the substance of the
faith or renounces its veracity, the heretic "does not abandon the
whole truth" but disfigures it.

Who is the God we worship?

Chapter Four

WHATEVER HAPPENED TO THE PECULIAR PEOPLE?

THE PARTISAN CAPTIVITY OF THE GOSPEL in the United States is the gravest theological crisis of the Christian faith in our time. I am certain that the story of American evangelicalism in the first decade of the twenty-first century will be studied by future generations of students and scholars as one of the most vivid examples of the church's cultural captivity in its two-thousand-year history. Cultural captivity comes about when the church constructs an image of God, either wittingly or unwittingly, on premises other than God's revelation of himself in Jesus Christ. Cultural captivity is not only a matter of Christians losing sight of their devotion to Jesus Christ. As Doctor Faustus sells his soul to Lucifer for twenty-four years of power, so evangelicals have gained much influence in the past decade as a result of their loyalty to conservative politics. But we have achieved access and power at the expense of the integrity of our witness.

No woman or man is capable of an uncompromised commitment to Christ. Certainly this fundamental fact must chasten all our judgments. We all sin and fall short of the glory of God. Still, our natural propensity toward ingratitude and disobedience is a matter different from our willful decision to graft the free and gracious word of God to the ambitions of a nation at war. We have profaned the faith's miraculous claims and sold them as commodities in the pursuit of our ambitions. Like the Protestant reformer Martin Luther, who protested "the pagan servitude of the Church"— the "idolaters" who had exchanged the freedom of God for the "ignorance, abuse, and mockery" of a corrupted hierarchy—we must now protest the political bondage of the gospel in the United States, the confessions and practices of a church that has reduced the cost of discipleship to the defense of cultural values, the preferences and wants of a paying clientele. We are not protesting the "gross superstitions of a masterful Rome" but the supreme arrogance of American Christendom.[1]

In the years 2000 to 2006, the gospel became so politicized in the United States—and by that I mean identified so closely by white evangelicals with the conservative Right—that the attempt to speak a distinctively Christian word was quite often construed as tendentiously liberal. It was a time when believers felt more comfortable saying "Jesus and America," "Jesus and moral values," "Jesus and principles for successful living"—always "Jesus and . . ." Not surprisingly, the attempt of dissenters to speak of the new social order of God appeared to the leaders of the politicized church as suspiciously out of step. Evangelical elites could be heard in the foyers and fellowship halls, on retreats and at private gatherings, insisting that a person could not be a Christian and a Democrat.

But eventually the truth of the gospel breaks free of propaganda and deception. Discipleship to Christ cannot be reduced to principles, values, and talking points, nor is it a matter of being fair and balanced. Costly discipleship begins with the humility that our ways are not God's ways and thus with patience and in obedience to God. Was the prophet Amos fair and balanced when he strolled in from Tekoa to declare that the Lord was roaring against the injustices of *all* the nations, including Israel, and not just her neighbors?

Why are we not then convening national conferences and stadium events asking difficult questions about our recent behavior, surveying the damage of our mistaken loyalty, weeping over our betrayals? Why are we not on bended knees together in prayer beseeching God for forgiveness, rededicating ourselves to the ministry of forgiveness and reconciliation? Why are we not filled with shame and broken hearts by the catastrophic consequences of our spiritual complicity in war and greed? We weep over Mel Gibson's *Passion of the Christ*; why are we not weeping over the devastation our own violence has unleashed on the innocent people of Iraq? We would rather talk about the evolution of the species, about how to become prosperous and happy, about effeminate and possibly gay cartoon characters, about taking Christ out of Christmas, about our fine contributions to culture, and about a million other matters. We would rather talk about anything, really, except the precise ways we have willfully offered up the gospel to the ravenous appetites of the state. But the effects of our bargain will not be hidden from the harsh light of history: The one question for which we will be forever accountable is why we exchanged the truth of God for political access and power.

The behavior of evangelical Christians in the United States presses an urgent question: Have we run our course and become finally indistinguishable from the American way of life? Have we betrayed the Bible's mandate "to do justly, and to love mercy, and to walk humbly with thy God" (Mic. 6:8 KJV)? Nothing less than this is at stake. In our haughty and promiscuous use of the language of faith, we have made it difficult to hear the word. Our noisiness has muted God's own speaking in our midst.

To be sure, evangelicals have gained intellectual respectability in recent decades, and we've won some battles in the culture wars and become more relevant and connected. We have gained access and influence. But at what cost? We seem to have forgotten that the gospel comes to us from a land far from our own. The word has been humiliated. We have humiliated the word. Where do we go from here?

The time is ripe for rededicating ourselves to being a peculiar people and to remember our primary mission of proclaiming salvation to the nations. I think it is also time to remember those men and women who have stood for Christ in unpopular ways, who live and speak out of complete trust in the word of God; it is time to call again upon the holy fools who proclaim the gospel through prayer and righteous action and in the sacrament of ordinary mercies. Not only is their witness a gift to us all, but their wisdom can fortify our own efforts and give us courage for the hard task at hand. Let us speak of those whose patriotism is first and foremost for God's kingdom, who harbor the victim and the outsider, who speak truth to power, who swim against the stream.

It is hard to be peculiar. The stories of Christian dissidents in our time often bring home the sobering lesson that those who follow the way of the cross should not expect to have many friends. In fact, dissent from the politicized gospel will often leave one in a lonely place. When the Southern Baptist progressive Clarence

Jordan died on a cold afternoon in late October 1969, he had been working in his one-room writing shack in the cornfields of Koinonia Farm, completing his *Cotton Patch Gospel of Matthew*. The county coroner refused to come and issue a death certificate, so the body of the preacher was driven into the town of Americus, Georgia, in the back of a station wagon. Jordan was buried the next afternoon in a cedar coffin dressed in his favorite pair of blue jeans; the white clergy and churchgoers from neighboring towns stayed home. Only fellow Koinonians, along with a few family members and black farmers, came to pay their final respects.

The stories of the church's saints, martyrs, and peacemakers are often hard to hear: They cut against the grain of success-driven religion and do not make good talking points for congregational success. The men and women who "refuse to remain spectators of the panorama of injustice," as Christopher Rowland writes in his study of radical Christianity, can expect to be "victims in conflicts with those who have the most to lose in the removal of injustice."[2] Living in the light of the cross and resurrection requires a little madness, no doubt, but such is the cost of discipleship. Let us then remember the peculiar people and reclaim the courage to be peculiar ourselves.

THE ONLY TIME I visited with the civil rights preacher Will D. Campbell, we sat on the porch of his Tennessee writing shack and shucked corn. We talked about his years as a Christian progressive in the segregated South and about what it meant then and now to live as "ambassadors of reconciliation."

Campbell was born in 1924 into a dirt-poor family in Amite

County, Mississippi, educated at Yale Divinity School, and ordained for the ministry in the Southern Baptist Convention. A
fondness for bourbon whisky, scatological language, and the radical orthodoxy of Karl Barth made him no more at home in the culturally conservative denomination than as a poor white Southerner
among the tweedy seminarians of Yale. Over the years, Campbell
would manage to infuriate just about every man and woman in the
South, segregationist and integrationist alike, starting with his one
term as the Director of Religious Life at Ole Miss.

Campbell began his ministry as a chaplain at the university in
the days following the Supreme Court's decision in *Brown v. Board,*
a time when McCarthyism and homegrown racism combined to
form a vicious paranoia throughout the Magnolia State. Agencies
like the Mississippi State Sovereignty Commission and the Citizens Council were created as guardians of white supremacy, vigi-
lantly monitoring the goings-on of outsiders and dissidents. The
white public was collectively, religiously devoted to the preserva-
tion of the southern way of life.

Campbell knew the world well. So he had no reason to be
shocked when his home was bombarded early one morning with
hundreds of ping-pong balls—some white, others painted black—
after he was seen playing the game with a black pastor visiting
the university. However, he knew there was great distress in the
soul of his fellow white Southerners when not long thereafter, at a
reception at the YMCA for the African American journalist Carl
Rowan, a pile of feces appeared in a bowl of non-alcoholic
punch, sprinkled with powdered sugar.[3] In 1955, Campbell was
fired from his position as a chaplain at Ole Miss for inviting
Alvin Kershaw to speak during the annual Religious Emphasis
Week. A white Episcopal priest from Ohio, Kershaw had become

a minor celebrity when he appeared on the popular television show *The $64,000 Question*. After winning $32,000 for successfully answering questions about jazz music, Kershall quit the show, saying he wanted to make sure he had money to donate to his favorite charities, which included the community chest, the 4-H Clubs, the American Red Cross, and the NAACP legal education and defense fund.[4] White Mississippians heard only the last, and since contributing to the NAACP was tantamount to making a public oath of allegiance to Russian communism, there was trouble afoot.

Campbell told me of a conversation he had had in the early sixties with several influential white clergymen at the Presbyterian seminary in Decatur, Georgia.[5] His book *Race and the Renewal of the Church*, published in 1962, had been stirring up intense debate in southern religious circles. Campbell had argued that the new identity of the Christian was one of complete and incontestable equality in Christ. "[The] Christian speaks as a member of a community which has never asked any question save the one concerning redemption," he said. "What do you think of Jesus?" Only one thing mattered in Campbell's view, that "God was in Christ reconciling the world to himself." Being a Christian meant joining a new family, "a *tertium genus*, a third race"—"a people neither Jew nor Greek, bond nor free, embracing master and slave alike, king and liege."[6] Racism has its roots in the sin of idolatry.

Campbell pushed the matter hard. Not only is membership in the Ku Klux Klan a betrayal of the gospel—most mainline white Christians would have had no trouble with that charge. The Klan could be dismissed as white trash and an embarrassment to the decent southern evangelical. But membership in the Country

Club is also a betrayal of the gospel, along with the Debutante Society, the Rotarians, the Kiwanians, the fraternities and sororities. But as a third race, a new people, Christians will need to decline membership in groups and organizations that separate by income, education, skin color, or cultural privilege. Years later, amidst much discussion in the early 1980s of the resurgence of white racist organizations in the United States, Campbell would warn liberals not to miss the bigger picture. "Let's talk about . . . the Ku Klux Klan," he said, "but let's do it in the context of the resurgence of Exxon and J. P. Stevens, and the resurgence of the Nashville's Belle Meade Country Club." Attempts to cling to the old ideal in any of its forms were a "living denial" of "the message of reconciliation entrusted to us."[7]

After his lecture at the Presbyterian seminary, Campbell was asked by a group of ministers to meet for an informal seminar. The men were disturbed by his application of the New Testament to southern race relations. Not wanting to address the race issue directly, however, the men said their purpose in meeting was to talk more about his theology.

"We want to know more about what you believe," one said.

Campbell replied that he'd just spent the better part of an hour telling them what he believed. But the ministers insisted there were matters that needed to be explored further.

So Campbell continued: "I was introduced in the chapel, but if you insist I'll tell you again. My name is Will D. Campbell. I am who my momma and daddy named me the night I was born. I live in Tennessee. I have three children. I am a preacher of the good news of Jesus Christ."

"Well, tell us about where you went to school," someone else demanded.

Campbell told them his schooling had nothing to do with the discussion. "You want to know who I am, what I believe? I'll tell you again. I believe God poured his love out for us in Jesus Christ, reconciled the world to himself, saved us from our sins. But I know why you're asking where I went to school. If I had gone to Bob Jones, that would mean one thing. If I went to the Presbyterian seminary, you'd think you'd know what that means. If I went to New Orleans Baptist Seminary, or Harvard, or Princeton, right away you'd think you'd know who I was. But the words are very clear in the scriptures. Once a man has truly seen the truth it doesn't matter where he's from, what his race is, or where he went to school. None of that matters."

One of the pastors who had fought in the Korean War wanted to hear more about Campbell's support of pacifism, which he'd mentioned in his talk. In the pastor's opinion there was no place for nonviolence in Christianity. "Just read the Old Testament and you'll see that God sometimes commands war," the man said. "I'm like the other pastors, Will. I just don't know what you believe."

By this point however Campbell had grown impatient. "Let me say it one more time," he said. "I believe God was in Christ, not maybe and not perhaps, not just if we're good boys and girls, but God was in Christ reconciling the world to himself. That means it's over and done with. Our salvation is accomplished. We are one people. We have been reconciled to God and to each other. And so racial prejudice is a violation of that fact. Nations are a violation; classes are a violation; joining the Country Club is a violation. I believe God was in Jesus Christ. Goddammit, that's what I believe!"

The last pastor who had spoken picked up his briefcase and headed briskly for the door.

"Where are you going?" Campbell asked.

"You think so much of Christ, but you certainly don't think too much of his father." The man's voice was shaking with anger.

"What are you talking about?"

"You took his name in vain. That's what I'm talking about," he said.

"I didn't take his name in vain," Campbell said. "I didn't take anybody's name in vain. Tell me how you think I took God's name in vain."

"I'm not saying anything more to you," the pastor said, standing in the doorway, looking at the Southern Baptist pastor in disbelief.

Finally one of the other ministers told his colleague, "Go ahead, tell Will he said 'goddammit.' It won't kill you."

But Campbell disagreed. "Do you really think I took the Father of Christ's name in vain? I don't think I did," he said. "Let's talk about what it means to take the Lord's name in vain. Every time a preacher quotes John 3:16 in the pulpit but does nothing to show love to the Negro, or every time he preaches from 2 Corinthians 5, but doesn't say that reconciliation applies directly to the race question, he's taking the name of God in vain. What do you think it means to take God's name in vain?"

"That's just semantics."

"You think so? I don't think so. I think every time someone says that man is made after the divine image, but promotes war and killing, he's taking the name of God in vain. What I'm saying is that you take God's name in vain every day of your life. You should at least have the decency to own up to the fact."[8]

After losing his job at Ole Miss, Campbell enlisted as a civil rights troubleshooter for the National Council of Churches. The year was 1957, and he was already recognized in progressive religious circles as the most visible white clergyman in the burgeoning civil rights movement. Campbell was the only white man involved in the creation of Martin Luther King Jr.'s Southern Christian Leadership Conference.[9] He walked with the Little Rock Nine, the African American students who sought to enroll in segregated Little Rock Central High School. "Here go nine children, defenseless, into God knows what," he said. "[I] simply fell in beside them."[10] Campbell put his life on the line time and again as an inside agitator and theological proponent of desegregation and racial reconciliation. He worked as a liaison to local authorities during civil rights demonstrations in Montgomery, Birmingham, New Orleans, Baton Rouge, Chattanooga, Fort Worth, and Richmond. These and many other acts of civil courage impressed not only the northern clergy but civil rights groups and social progressives of all religious persuasions.

Still, Campbell understood that the ministry of reconciliation to which he had been called made him peculiar in the eyes of the world, and as he pursued his vocation in the changing South, he became increasingly convinced that Christ-shaped love resisted identification with either conservative or liberal politics. In 1963 he scandalized many in the movement when he announced that the same concern that they had been showing to the disenfranchised minority should be shown to poor whites, segregationists, and racists. Many of these men and women, who were unsettled by the prospects of legal equality for blacks, had been abused as children and were tormented by fears and uncontrollable rage, often by untreated mental illness. Campbell made himself available as pastor and confessor to racists and to members of the Ku Klux Klan, seeking to share gospel-grace with outcasts and sinners.

"Most of us suspect that if Christ came back today he would once again be born among the lowly," he explained. "But wouldn't it shake us up if he came today and was born into a Klan family!"[11] The redneck racist needed to be loved and cared for. Such was the radical love of Christ, the spirit of *agape.*

The National Council of Churches began requiring Campbell to submit his articles and speeches to its New York office in advance of his public appearances, a requirement which, needless to say, he did not receive graciously. At the 1963 Centennial Conference on Religion and Race in Chicago, which the NCC hoped would be a defining moment for the progressive Protestant movement, Campbell prepared a speech with lines that read, "If I live to be as old as my father, I expect to see whites marched into the gas chambers, the little children clutching their toys to their breasts in Auschwitz fashion, at the hands of a black Eichmann."[12] Conference organizers were furious. The doctrine of human depravity might be biblically sound, but it surely did not make good publicity for cold war religious liberals hoping to be taken seriously in the modern social order. Campbell's remark seemed outrageously irresponsible.

"[Sin] is no respecter of persons," he said in defense. "The problem of injustice in America cannot be reduced to Birmingham, Jackson, and Atlanta, to the problem of segregation in the South; the problem of injustice is Chicago, New Haven, and Boston, to all of America. The problem is human sinfulness."

"That's fine," an official responded. "And you can believe that back in Tennessee."[13]

Campbell agreed to cut the remark, though he was left with the nagging sense that something had gone wrong when Christians began speaking of racists and rednecks as enemies. A Christian was not free to pick and choose his or her friends and enemies; the born-again mission meant loving the other in grace and without conditions. "We're all bastards but God loves us anyway," was the way Campbell came to sum up the gospel. The mercies of Christ finally overwhelm all hostility and prejudice.

Campbell explained the peculiar mission of the southern Christian radical in a 1965 letter to his friend, novelist Walker Percy:

> We think the issues are theological, not just social or political. We do not oppose the invading moral carpetbaggers (we had it coming) except as we are aware of history and try to understand that love means trust and that if we are to follow our Lord we must hope and work also for white Southerners—not just seek to force them. We are trying to distinguish between integration and reconciliation—[and] what more than that can we Christians do? We are concerned with the primitive heretical socio-theology of the crusaders as well as the crawl of the Church, but we do not see ourselves as having the answers in our hands.[14]

These are not views that can be easily assimilated into a story of good guys against bad. For the question remains how to witness to "our Lord" in a changing social order without mistaking our personal imperatives for the gospel mission.

IN AUGUST OF 1998, Campbell traveled to Hattiesburg, Mississippi, for the trial of Sam Bowers. Bowers was the former Imperial Wizard of the White Knights of the Ku Klux Klan of Mississippi, who reigned over the most violent white terrorist organization in the South. He orchestrated the 1964 murders of James Chaney, Andrew Goodman, and Michael Schwerner, which riveted the nation and brought massive media attention to the state's brutal racism; in 1998, more than thirty years after his first arrest, Bowers was convicted for the 1966 murder of Vernon Dahmer, an NAACP leader, land owner, and churchman in Forrest County, Mississippi. Campbell had been introduced to Bowers in the time of his impending arrest, when Bowers was still living in the nearby town of Laurel, running a pinball machine company and writing tracts on politics and religion.[15] Only a few people knew of Campbell's pastoral relationship with the Klansman, which lasted until his death in Parchman Prison on November 5, 2006.

On the first day of the trial, Campbell arrived early in the Hattiesburg courthouse and approached Bowers, who was sitting at the defendant's table, and shook his hand. Bowers asked the minister to take a seat but Campbell declined. Campbell then walked across the room, greeted the Dahmer family, and took a seat with them, where he remained for the rest of the day.

During a recess in the trial, a newspaper reporter asked Campbell how it was possible for him to walk between the grieving family and the Klan terrorist, who surely deserved punishment, not compassion. Campbell's actions seemed offensive to the reporter. Did he really think Bowers deserved his kindness? Most newspaper coverage had portrayed Bowers as a monster, the embodiment of pure evil.

The Southern Baptist preacher adjusted his black frame glasses and offered an explanation to the Boston journalist, a variation on his earlier "This I Believe" speech, an updated testimonial of his strange vocation. Why had he acknowledged Sam Bowers with a handshake? "It's just because I'm a goddamned

Christian," he said. He would be sitting with the Dahmer family, but as a minister of the gospel, he would not forsake Bowers, even though the former Imperial Wizard was wholly undeserving of such love.

The last time I talked to Will, I asked him if he was still preaching at the little church near his farm in Mount Joliette, Tennessee. He drawled out a "no" and said he had long gotten tired of the "steeple." Besides, he added, the standing invitation to preach had been withdrawn, a result no doubt of some contrary remark, though I didn't press for details. When I asked Will where he was going to church, he told me he'd decided to become a "seventh day horizontalist," and we both laughed. He has earned the time off.

LET US TEACH OUR CHILDREN the story of Will Campbell and all the other Jesus-loving misfits, oddballs, and malcontents who rub against the grain. For it will surely not be the court prophets, patriot preachers, and right-wing megalomaniacs whose stories the church will tell young people as exemplars of authentic faith. The philosopher Friedrich Nietzsche once said that Christians must sing more beautiful songs before he would believe in their redeemer.[16] We will need to sing more beautiful songs to our children and to the world.

Let us speak of those who stand for God in the quiet work of justice and mercy. Let us speak of the reconcilers, the peacemakers, and the brokenhearted—of those who long, the mad, and the maladjusted. There are many in the United States and throughout the world who labor quietly in inauspicious places restoring hope among the disheartened and the excluded; we find them serving food to the hungry, sharing their evenings with the lonely and forgotten, showing hospitality to strangers, building houses for the homeless, encouraging all those who despair with words of healing and kindness. Sometimes too we find them in their writing shacks crafting stories of the new kingdom. These people are like wild and crooked trees. They live in the freedom of Christ with open hearts and minds. They are rough around the edges but real as rock.

The Roman Catholic intellectual Michael Budde has noted, in his observations on cultural Christianity in America, that "we in the advanced industrial world find ourselves less able to sustain *any* life-forming narrative that is recognizably Christian."[17] Budde laments the absence of "passion" in our consumer-driven Christian culture, the absence of wholehearted commitment to live inside the story of the "life, mission, and message of the Anointed One." Budde does not mean the kind of passion popular in American religious culture, mass-marketed in films, festivals, and rallies. Budde means rather a passion for the total truth of the gospel.

Too many Christians in North America—Catholic and Protestant alike—gaze upon the Christian moral tradition with the indifference of spoiled children. It is the brokering for access and the flash of notoriety that excites us—and that conveniently excuses the gospel from making any difference in our view of the world. But other than the historical peace churches—the Mennonites, the Christian Brethren, the Quakers—and the Catholic social tradition—there is no longer a viable tradition of Christian dissent in American Christian culture, and thus there is no real passion. "Indifference to the Gospel . . . is the greatest danger to the church today," Budde writes.[18] Living passionately for the gospel, on the other hand, means reckoning with the theological significance of our baptisms, the beginning of new life in Christ, and thus learning to live in the community of Christ as the place in the world where the world finds the hope it cannot find elsewhere.

There was a time when evangelicals in the United States were encouraged to accept their status as a marginal people, and the description was not meant as a complaint about our modest cultural influence. We embraced the identity as a mark of our mission in the world. Our life together as believers was linked with the story of Israel, chosen by the Lord, as the book of Deuteronomy says, "to be a peculiar people unto himself" (14:2 KJV). We heard the call to be peculiar as a call to be set apart from the nations, and although we no doubt often expressed our set-apartness in narrowly moralistic terms—in teetotaling, or abstinence from dance, cards, movies, and the carnal pleasures—we nonetheless knew that Christian faithfulness meant living against the grain of the world before it meant taking a seat at the Congressional Prayer Breakfast.

In the First Epistle of Saint Peter, the followers of Christ are also called to be "a peculiar people," and this people should show forth "the praises of him who hath called you out of darkness into his marvelous light" (1 Pet. 2:9 KJV). We must take care when studying this lesson and appropriating its meaning in our lives, for the peculiarity of the Christian is not a quality in which we can boast, as in the notion that we are chosen because we *are* the special people. The New Testament book of First Peter echoes the Old Testament books of Deuteronomy and especially Exodus, where we find Moses proclaiming God's hope for Israel: "Now therefore, if ye will obey my voice indeed, and keep my covenant, then ye shall be a peculiar treasure unto me above all people: for all the earth is mine" (19:5 KJV). Much is expected of those who call upon the name of the Lord. The people who keep the covenant will be peculiar.

This is what it means to keep the covenant. Being peculiar and being chosen—a "royal priesthood" and a "holy nation"—means being a people who practice mercy and seek justice. Only the nation that defends the defenseless, establishes equity, and relieves the oppressed is "chosen." This is the message of the prophets.

In the early Christian document *St. Mathetes Epistle to Diognetus*, we encounter a series of fascinating observations about the new community gathering around the message of Jesus Christ. The letter was drafted in the early second century and written in the fashion of Saint Paul's letters. Some scholars have argued that Mathetes was a catechumenate or associate of the great apostle of the Lord.

The ancient document ponders the questions: Who are the Christians? What God do they trust? By what standard do they live their lives? Or as Mathetes himself asks, "What is the affection which they cherish among themselves?" The answers offer a glimpse into the moral universe of these Jesus-followers. Clearly the Christians do not live as the pagans. They do not worship idols. They do not worship God through superstition or through the spilling of animal blood and the "smoke of sacrifices and burnt offerings." The Christians do not worship gods made by hand. Neither are they distinguished by the country in which they live or the customs they keep. Rather, the Christians, inhabiting Greek and barbarian cities, remaining fully in the places of their birth, display "a wonderful and confessedly striking method of life."[19] The Christians are marked by a distinctive manner and style.

As we read in the *Epistle*:

> For they dwell not somewhere in cities of their own, neither do they use some different language, nor practise an extraordinary kind of life.
>
> Nor again do they possess any invention discovered by any intelligence or study of ingenious men, nor are they masters of any human dogma as some are.
>
> But while they . . . follow the native customs in dress and food and the other arrangements of life, yet the constitution of their own citizenship, which they set forth, is marvellous, and confessedly contradicts expectation.
>
> They dwell in their own countries, but only as sojourners; they bear their share in all things as citizens, and they endure all hardships as strangers. Every foreign country is a fatherland to them, and every fatherland is foreign.
>
> They marry like all other men and they beget children; but they do not cast away their offspring.
>
> They have their meals in common, but not their wives.
>
> They find themselves in the flesh, and yet they live not after the flesh.
>
> Their existence is on earth, but their citizenship is in heaven.
>
> They obey the established laws, and they surpass the laws in their own lives.
>
> They love all men, and they are persecuted by all.
>
> They are ignored, and yet they are condemned.
>
> They are put to death, and yet they are endued with life.
>
> They are in beggary, and yet they make many rich. They are in want of all things, and yet they abound in all things.
>
> They are dishonoured, and yet they are glorified in their

dishonour. They are evil spoken of, and yet they are vindicated.

They are reviled, and they bless; they are insulted, and they respect.

Doing good they are punished as evil-doers; being punished they rejoice, as if they were thereby quickened by life.[20]

It is time for Christians in the United States to live again like strangers in a strange land. This does not require our withdrawal from the world or disengagement from politics and culture. It means that we learn to act and to think, to read and to interpret, to organize and to vote, out of the new light springing from the gospel. It means bearing witness to the authenticity of our faith and building hope in the practices we keep: showing hospitality to strangers and outcasts; affirming the unity of the created order; reclaiming the ideals of beauty, love, honesty, and truth; and embracing the preferential option for nonviolence. It means learning to live in the world in a way that is participatory rather than manipulative, living in expectation of a time when we may speak of God once more as one who comes to us from a country far from our own.

"These things I have spoken to you," Jesus says in Saint John's gospel, "that in Me you may have peace. In the world, you will have tribulation; but be of good cheer; I have overcome the world" (16:33 NKJV).

Chapter Five

THEOLOGY MATTERS
Including a Brief History of Modern Christianity in Which the Reader Learns Why the Christian Right Are Theological Liberals

THERE WAS ONCE A TIME when religious scholars took part in the critical issues of the day. The great American public theologians of the mid-twentieth century, Reinhold Niebuhr and Paul Tillich, were both featured on the cover of *Time* magazine, and their articles and essays appeared in major newspapers and magazines, as well as in academic and political journals. Their books were often published by the leading trade houses. Paul Tillich may have tried too hard to accommodate modern secular culture, as Niebuhr and Barth both believed, but his probing meditations on alienation and anxiety, his creative use of Augustine, Luther, Freud, and Heidegger, along with his numerous trendy cultural avocations, put him at the intellectual center of a generation of forward-thinking church people and students.

Niebuhr called his own work an "apologetics," by which he had in mind the defense and justification of the Christian faith for a secular age. Niebuhr recast the whole catalog of Christian doctrine as lessons in political humility and civil courage. In his concept of "Christian realism," Niebuhr intended to remind modern believers that there never will be any "final escape in historic existence from the contradictions in which human nature is involved." His honest assessments of power and justice struck a chord with people searching for a way beyond liberal idealism and Victorian quietism, beyond utopianism and resignation. "The Christian stands between the illusions and the despair of the world," he said.[1]

Then there was Karl Barth, the Swiss professor of Dogmatic Theology who single-handedly revitalized the language of orthodoxy in the modern world. Barth was also pictured on the cover of *Time*. In the April 20, 1962, issue, the intense face of the seventy-five-year-old theologian is set against the empty tomb of Jesus Christ, where a crown of thorns has been cast aside on Easter morning. A banner at the top right of the cover reads: "The goal of human life is not death, but resurrection."

The days of the public theologian are over. There is no longer a representative mainline Protestant voice, as there is no longer any identifiable mainline Protestant culture. This is not to say that theology has fallen on hard times; many theologians in the academy own the skills to bridge the two worlds and speak to a public audience. Sadly, only a few who have the skills seek to engage a larger conversation. In any case, the sound bites of the religious celebrities are clearly preferred by the public to the writings of the theologians, whose reliance on bipartite and tripartite distinctions and dialectical habits of speech discourages the easy read.

The forecasts for a secular America made amidst the social crises of the 1960s, most notably by Harvard theologian Harvey Cox in his influential 1965 book, *The Secular City,* have not played out to script. Cox predicted the coming of a "secular epoch" that would liberate humankind from "its religious and metaphysical tutelage."[2] More than forty years later, the very notion of the secular is under daily assault by religious groups across the spectrum of belief. We find ourselves in a nation of intense spiritual obsessions—abuzz with religious energies, with faith-based writing, commentary, and activism—and in a world saturated in religious fervor. The evangelical media market alone is a billion-dollar industry. The public debate often feels as if it is "all God all the time," and Cox's "new era of urban secularity" seems now like the wishful thinking of a disenchanted churchman.[3] His 1995 book, *Fire from Heaven: The Rise of Pentecostal Spirituality and the Reshaping of Religion in the Twenty-First Century*, is an illuminating study of the global Pentecostal movement, and in this way a retraction of his youthful take on the *zeitgeist*.

In fact, theology matters now more than ever, and it will not do to wish that we all go away, as inevitable—or desirable—as that might seem to some. The theologian needs to be heard in the public conversation on religion and politics and by pastors and laity in the churches. While there are new movements in the guild that deserve broader attention, the reason we need theology now has less to do with its contemporary vitality than with its time-honored practice of restoring discipline and carefulness to religious speech. Too many of us in the Christian community have forgotten that we stand in a tradition of careful thinking and articulation, that there are intellectual demands that come in confessing Christ, rules of speech and reasoning. At its best, theology has a way of slowing down language, interrupting easy formulas, unsettling partisan confidences, and disciplining thought.

Can anyone doubt that the churches in the United States could use a little more theology and a lot less religious talk?

THE GREAT KARL BARTH DEFINES THEOLOGY as the "self-examination of the Christian church in respect of the content of its distinctive talk about God."[4] The important features of his definition are worth noting. "Self-examination" is the courage to ask critical and non-defensive questions of the way the community speaks the language of faith. "The Christian church" highlights the theologian's commitment to serve the fellowship of faith, local and global. "Distinctive talk about God" refers to the conviction that the Christian community has a peculiar grammar and logic, an inner sense, if you will, grounded in the revelation of God in Jesus Christ. It might be a hard lesson for Christians in America to learn, but thinking Christianly means thinking in terms of inherited rules and guidelines. Christians have intellectual obligations. Jesus prayed "Our Father who art in heaven, hallowed be thy name" as a way of teaching his disciples how to address God and order their thoughts. He was not trying to inhibit freedom of expression but to give freedom an appropriate form.

There is ample room for thinking creatively, and freely, inside a generous orthodoxy. Orthodoxy, as I know it, much more than modernism, unlocks faith's intricate and ennobling perceptions, and frames all that exceeds our grasping, is the desire, hunger, love, mystery, and beauty. Still, there are rules or patterns that determine whether theological thinking has remained (generously) orthodox and faithful to Scripture and tradition. Christians must be more romantic than the romanticist, more human than the humanist, Karl Barth once said, but Christians must be more precise. These rules or patterns enable freedom; they awaken thought's fullness and complexity.

However, I am not concerned here with the exposition of church doctrines. I direct the reader to any of the sixteen volumes in Barth's *Church Dogmatics* for a systematic presentation of Christian revelation. My point is to note that historic Christianity is about faithfulness to the distinctive truth claims of the faith and obedience to God; it is not about the convictions of nations, cultures, and folk traditions. In contemporary religious culture, there is much talk about Christian values and principles but precious little self-examination or searching after the distinctive speech and practices of the gospel. This dearth of theological thinking is serious business. The Presbyterian scholar John Leith wrote in the preface to his essential anthology, *The Creeds of the Churches: A Reader in Christian Doctrine from the Bible to the Present*, that "No pretheological era has been discovered in the New Testament or in the history of the Christian community."[5] From its earliest origins, Christianity has been a theological faith, involving men and women in theological thinking and calling them to affirmations and declarations of belief. "A nontheological Christianity has simply never endured," Leith says, "although such has been attempted, for instance, by individual seers (*Spiritualisten*) in the sixteenth century and also by collaborators with totalitarian ideologies (e.g., the *positives Christentum* of the German Christians) in the twentieth century."

That strikes me as an exceedingly important point. The popular preacher and best-selling author Joel Osteen said he is not interested in theology but in practical things. Pastor Osteen seems to me like a very likable man. I appreciate his ministry of encouragement, his gentle and soft-spoken manner. But Christianity was rooted in the theological traditions of ancient Israel, which was unified by its historical credos and affirmations of faith. If Christians ignore theology, refuse self-examination, or fail to consider the distinctive truth claims of the faith, then we will have unanchored ourselves from the shore of revelation and history.

Thinking carefully about God matters. For one reason, God created persons in God's image and thus as intelligent beings. The human being is *intelligens*, the one who understands, the intelligent being; therefore, the Christian must be able to discern with "agonizing clarity" all that it means to confess God as creator of all things, the true and the beautiful. While we should not entrap faith within the limits of human reason, we must still be unwavering in our conviction that faith means "neither the closing of the mind nor the sacrifice of the integrity of the mind." As Christians, we acknowledge our intellectual obligations not only to be prepared with a reasonable account of our beliefs but also to speak to each other in language that honors the majesty and mystery of the triune God.

A second reason is that the Christian faith claims that God is truth, the author and source of truth. A commitment to God that fails to honor God with the whole mind is as dangerous as it is irresponsible and irreverent. Speaking of God intelligently and charitably is an essential condition of spiritual growth and discernment. Although Christians may often act otherwise, thinking intelligently, and thinking intelligently about God is no less basic to discipleship than spiritual devotion and compassionate service. In a time such as ours, when the name of Jesus has been offered to the highest bidder, judicious and careful thought must be reaffirmed as a basic obligation of every person who assents to the truth claims of the gospel.

In an address given in March of 1933, less than two months after Hitler became Chancellor of Germany, Karl Barth proposed a way of thinking about the rules and patterns of Christian theology that may help us in our time. He referred to the first commandment, "thou shalt have no other gods before me," as the basic axiom of Christian speech and practice. The first commandment is the "absolutely fundamental and foundational presupposition of theology," he said.[6] The commandment issues a permanent and unassailable reminder that none of us controls God, and that true piety always resists the temptation to lay claim to the holy.

From beginning to end, Barth's writings read like a hymn of praise. His arguments, compositions, and excursions are brimming with joy for the risen Christ. Everywhere there is gladness for the God who has come to redeem and befriend humanity. I regard Barth as the foremost evangelical theologian of the modern era, a prince of the church who devoted his life to the task of revitalizing the whole structure of Christian doctrine, which had steadily crumbled beneath the weight of modernity. The Yale theologian Hans Frei once said that Barth's achievement was to restate or reconstitute "a language that had once been accustomed talk, both in first-order use in ordinary or real life, and in second-order technical reflection, but had now for a long time . . . been receding from natural familiarity."[7] We should also not forget that if Karl Barth were alive today, taking part in our public debates on religion and political responsibility (as he would be), he would undoubtedly find himself stigmatized by the religious right as a left-wing foreigner and bullied accordingly. Barth's reminder that no nation can embody the righteousness of God and that "the Gospel is not one thing in the midst of other things . . . but the Word, which, since it is ever new, must ever be received with renewed fear and trembling" is quite unsettling to those who seek to wed the Christian faith and American values.[8] For too many of us have found it easier to place our hopes in "Jesus and moral values," "Jesus and the market," and "Jesus and America" without concern for what the "and" may be doing to our confession of Jesus as Lord over all creation.

The behavior of Christians in the U.S. has reached this strange place, where exuberant Christian orthodoxy sounds to some altogether un-American, or at least suspiciously leftist, where attempts to speak of social and political existence in distinctively Christian terms sound tendentiously radical (as they sometimes are!). Barth reminds us that genuine Christian thought humbles itself before the first commandment as it lives in steady mindfulness of our idolatrous proclivities. "I think and speak with theological responsibility," he said, "when I know myself to be responsible to that commandment in what I think and speak as a theologian . . . 'You shall have no other gods before me!' "[9]

There is a remarkable theological irony in the theological habits of the Christian Right, which is entirely lost on the secular and religious media, but which I wish to note here: Every time we hear the voice of the Christian nationalist, or the claims, implicit or direct, that God is on our side, or such boasts as, "We teach patriotism as being synonymous with Christianity" (Falwell), or "America is a Christian nation" (General William Boykin), we are in fact hearing the voice (unwittingly, perhaps, but unmistakably) of the Protestant liberal tradition.[10] These liberal sentiments accompany all the noisy talk about Christian principles and Christian values; they are based on a way of thinking about God (a method, as the teachers say) that has its historical roots in the Protestant liberal tradition of nineteenth-century European intellectual thought. It strikes me as a noteworthy turn of events that our patriot preachers and court prophets remain our most zealous proponents of the liberal theological tradition. Understanding why this is the case requires some explanation.

The terms "liberal" and "conservative," as they are tossed around in our public debates, are not meaningful as descriptions of Christian faith and practice, even though many conservatives would have us believe that the terms can be transferred willy-nilly from their popular political use to religion. In fact, biblical Christianity, along with the history of Christian theology and ethics, resists this move. Jim Wallis writes that faith challenges politics "from a consistent moral ground," and that "God's politics" challenges "national, ethnic, economic, or cultural self-interest," thus reminding us of a "much wider world and the creative human diversity of all those made in the image of the creator."[11]

Supporting a tax increase that provides services for the poor, to take one timely example, ought not be regarded as a "liberal" notion from the perspective of Christian social teaching. In 2004, the Republican governor of Alabama, Bob Riley, after reading a report by a University of Alabama law professor on the plight of the poor in the state, a situation made continually worse by unfair tax codes, began a personal study on the Bible and poverty. Riley discovered that an honest engagement with Scripture, from the book of Genesis to the book of Revelation, presents an image of God who expects his people to care for the poor and protect the "little ones."[12] In Scripture, God continually announces his favor on the impoverished and the oppressed. The Bible contains more than 2,000 references to the poor. Israel was called to be a compassionate nation, and the Christian story begins with the birth of the Savior, homeless in a manger, who takes the side of "the least of these." Governor Riley reached the conclusion that his state's tax code violated Judeo-Christian teachings on poverty and social justice, and his proposals to revise the code in more equitable terms were eventually signed into law in the spring of 2006, despite an initial defeat and the protests of both the Alabama Christian Coalition and Grover Norquist's non-Christian anti-tax operation. Although the new law fell short of its original design to cut taxes on the poor by raising revenues on the wealthy, it still represented a concrete realization of the Republican governor's struggle to apply biblical social teachings to the alleviation of poverty and economic misery.

One of the strengths of Wallis's book is that it demonstrates the moral narrowness that has led to political impasse. Public life in the United States, Wallis writes, is a "bankrupt battlefield of competing special interests without the framework of moral discourse," and moral issues become too easily politicized without attention to their distinctive meaning in the Judeo-Christian tradition.[13] Further, the pacifist tradition (in its Protestant forms) in the United States and its ethics of nonviolence have been sustained largely through the efforts of Mennonites, Christian Brethren, Quakers, and other members of the historic peace churches, traditions that are deeply influenced by the radical Reformation as well as by the teachings of the ancient church, especially the doctrine of *imitatio Christi*, as found in such classic works as Thomas à Kempis's *Imitation of Christ*, *The Little Flowers of St. Francis of Assisi*, and

Athanasius's *Life of Antony*. Affirming the sacred value of created life ought not to be regarded as a "conservative" position insofar as it consistently covers the whole ethics of life from unborn to infirm to criminal, as Pope John Paul II made the case in his encyclical *Evangelium Vitae*.

The point is not to sift through the conflicting and contradictory notions of liberal and conservative in their popular use but to note that historic Christianity resists partisan captivity and illuminates a different social framework. My point is also to say that in their hesitation to move from the former to the latter, those who represent the Christian Right become theological liberals unaware. Protestant liberalism built its franchise on the premise that the truth claims of Christianity could be recast in a manner consistent with the secularizing drift of the modern world. The claims and doctrines of the faith could be made palatable for men and women who had outgrown the need for a supernatural crutch.

THE STORY OF MODERN THEOLOGY begins with Immanuel Kant and his two devastating books, *The Critique of Pure Reason* and *The Critique of Practical Reason*. In these trenchant analyses of the human mind and its organization of experience, Kant reached a conclusion that dramatically influenced all subsequent theological and philosophical thought in the West. He claimed that the idea of God is uncertain and unknowable, since it does not appear in space and time; thus, God's existence cannot be known with the certainty of objective (that is, empirical) knowledge.[14] To be sure, the idea of God remains useful in providing order to moral experience, but the idea, stripped of its objective reference, can no longer be regarded as reliable in the realm of natural reason.

The story of Protestant liberalism begins with this momentous adaptation: Metaphysical reality, the doctrines and beliefs of the church, are meaningful only as lessons that help organize human experience in ethically beneficial ways. As for being descriptions of the triune God, the one who is Father, Son, and Holy Spirit, who on the third day raised Jesus Christ from the dead, and all the rest—the doctrines and beliefs of the church are empty of objective meaning. The greatest liberal theologian of the era, Friedrich Schleiermacher, in his beautiful book *On Religion: Speeches to Its Cultured Despisers*, may have shown us that Kant's reduction could engender inspired results, as in Schleiermacher's exquisite rendering of religion as an aesthetic sensibility, "a sense and taste for the Infinite." Nevertheless, the damage was done as far as the substance of Christian belief was concerned.[15] The claims of the faith, which before the Enlightenment had been considered the most truthful reality, would be hereafter considered in a deeply suspicious light.

Following Kant, the radical critiques of religion developed by Ludwig Feuerbach, Karl Marx, and Sigmund Freud in the nineteenth and twentieth centuries demonstrated the far-reaching consequences of the intellectual shift. Feuerbach claimed that the beliefs of the Christian faith are human projections; afraid to acknowledge their unbounded potential, humans naïvely project their own infinite value onto a transcendent screen and name that image God. Marx called religion an "opiate of the masses," a force that constrains freedom and keeps the working masses servile. From his vantage point in the analyst's chair, Freud diagnosed religion as a neurotic symptom, a "universal obsessional neurosis," which might be relieved by greater self-knowledge. In this manner, Schleiermacher's definition of religion as the "holy wedlock of the Universe with the incarnated Reason for a creative, productive embrace" was just what a psychoanalyst should expect of a north German Pietist with a hankering for maternal intimacy.[16] Religion, at its best, helps emotionally feeble men cope with irrational forces. These three radical critiques share the view that questions about human nature and experience are finally answered more honestly in secular and scientific accounts.

Thus, the liberal Protestant tradition, inasmuch as it claims that knowledge of God must be based on some mode or dimension of human experience (beauty, moral order, inner bliss, political loyalty) leads to a theological dead end. Indeed it leads to the conclusion that God is but an extension of human experience, a projection of human need and longing. Barth, whose neo-orthodox theology arose as a protest against this tradition, said that Protestant liberalism led to the mistake of "speaking about God by speaking about humanity in a loud voice."[17] The liberal theologians tried so hard to accommodate the gospel to the modern world that they ended up surrendering the faith "to the patterns, forces, and movements of human history and civilization"—and to an "uncritical and irresponsible subservience" to these patterns, forces, and movements.[18] The Christian gospel was changed into a principle of purpose, a set of moral values, and a cultural or political program, and the ship of the church drifted aimlessly into perilous waters.

What does all this have to do with the situation of churches in the United States? When the conservative religious elites speak of the Christian nation, Christian principles, Christian values, or Christian prosperity in quasi-theological language, they are standing firmly in the tradition of Protestant liberalism. In this

way, the conservative Christian elites have become the new
Protestant liberals: Christ is the projection and guarantor of our
values, ambitions, and power. The cross of Jesus is the symbol of
our political ideals rather than the place of ultimate agony on
which God exploded into time and defeated Satan's power. In the
harrowing photograph of the political organizers in Ohio, Bush
and Cheney have literally shoved Jesus off the cross. Reading the
war sermons reaffirms the basic liberal conviction that Jesus' life
and teachings cannot be taken seriously for political existence in
the modern world.

A return to exuberant Christian conviction must then begin
with the sober recognition that Christ comes to us from a country
far from our own. And that fallen humanity, which is to say all
humanity, is brought into fellowship with God solely as a gift of
God's unconditional love, shown in Jesus' saving journey to the
hill of ultimate sorrow. Our acceptance of God's invitation to the
fellowship of his love begins only when we lay our values, traditions, and habits at the foot of the cross. John Calvin said we
must "cleave unto God" so that our unholy nature will be infused
with God's holiness and we are then able to live as his worthy children.[19] God knows us before we know ourselves, and that knowledge must reshape our perception of life.

IT HAS HAPPENED A FEW TIMES in recent years that a politician or
journalist has invoked the Nazi regime as a comparison to the
policies of the current administration. In every instance, the comparison has elicited prompt and wide-ranging denunciations, as
it should, and the accuser has offered a public apology. While
political comparisons between German Nazism and American

democracy are fairly absurd, I confess to the strong urge to make theological comparisons. Certainly there are enormous and significant differences between the two idolatrous churches—the jingoistic tones of American conservative Christianity and the nazified church of the Third Reich—and I find tiresome in the extreme the efforts of certain members of the left to collapse differing and discrete historical situations in order to craft one great cautionary tale about American empire.

Nevertheless, Christians around the world have learned important lessons about the confusion of religious loyalties by studying the story of the German church. There is simply no greater example of disfigured Christianity in modern church history, and thus the comparative question must be raised. The question should not be raised to score political points but as part of an honest and healthy self-examination of our work and witness. One might even regard these hard questions as ingredients of the spiritual discipline of "walking circumspectly," "not as fools but as wise people," sober-minded and judicious, as Saint Paul encourages Christians in their pursuit of a transformed mind and testimony marked by the cross (Eph. 5:17 KJV). Reckoning honestly with the heresy of the *deutsche Christen* also involves accepting Christianity's deep complicity in evil. The license given by the churches to exterminate the Jews may have been a product of a twisted cross, but it was a Christian distortion, not a secular humanist or Muslim distortion. The church lives forever with the obligation to evaluate its witness in the searching light of its past failures. We do not have an exemption from probing self-criticism, and, moreover, we undermine the credibility of our witness when we willfully ignore the faith's endorsement throughout the centuries of immoral campaigns and unjust regimes.

The German nation considered itself the apotheosis of Western civilization. The nineteenth-century philosopher Gottlieb Fichte wrote in his lumbering *Addresses to the German Nation* that "the German spirit . . . will open up new shafts and bring the light of day into their abysses, and hurl up rocky masses of thoughts, out of which ages to come will build their dwellings."[20] Fichte, like many of his contemporaries, believed that an organic, if not a metaphysical, relation existed between the life of God and the essence of Germany. Christian leaders played a vital role in promoting the ideas of the *Volk* and *Vaterland* in a unifying spiritual vision, which gave birth to the world-threatening German ethnocentrism.[21] Some theologians argued in support of a "disinheritance theory," boasting that Christianity cancelled God's election of the Jews and thus abolished their inheritance of the covenant; this theological boast cleared the way for that of *Deutschland über alles.*

Others argued that Jesus should no longer be regarded as a Jew, or that the New Testament should be deracinated from the Hebrew Bible. Once Christianity had been stripped of its Jewishness, it was an easy step to think of Jesus as a blue-eyed, blond-haired German male and the German nation as God's chosen favorite. As the Canadian scholar Alan Davies explained in his remarkable book, *Infected Christianity: A Study of Modern Racism*, "More and more, the Aryan Christ became a synonym for the essential divinity of Aryan man. . . . [C]lothed in Aryan dress, and elevated to the status of white German tribal deity, [Jesus] was the perfect religious symbol of a racist church in a totalitarian state."[22] Not only did the German *Volk*, with its quasi-religious notions of home and hearth and its veneration of Aryan family values, become the standard for thinking properly about Christian faith and practice, but these ideas further gave shape to a hideous conception of human nature. There were precious few voices of dissent among the ranks of the pious and the churchly.

Numerous questions raised in the German story need to be addressed to our own time and place. Do Christians in the United States possess the skills of interpretation and discernment that would have enabled us to defy the nazified church and its demands for total loyalty? Do we have the theological tools to name, and then to resist, the idols? Are we equipped with the convictions and perceptions that would have inspired resistance to the nation's claims for soul-allegiance and supreme devotion? Would we have been able to avoid the lure of the Aryan Christ, recognize this Christ as a false god, or as an antichrist? I keep thinking of Jerry Falwell's remark that "our God is pro-war," or Charles Stanley's plea to support the war effort by any means possible, or Franklin Graham's image of the warrior Jesus, and of the obsequious nod of the evangelical elites to the White House and the Pentagon.

If we believe that our way of life, values, traditions, and nation are essential to God's providence, blessed above all the nations, then we have *already* crossed the line from confessing Christ as Lord to incarcerating Christ in our own ideological gulags. If we demur on the total claim of the gospel on our lives, we will soon produce national myths and religious constructions that serve only to celebrate our preferences and ambitions. History teaches us the lesson time and again: We dare not try to evade its lessons by claiming that America is somehow different from all the others. If we are convinced that God is on our side, then we will be inclined in every instance to overlook our own propensities towards cruelty and injustice. Our hold on spiritual supremacy will authorize acts of aggression and violence, which we will deem useful in preserving our way of life and our religious ideals, and most of what we do in defense of ourselves will be justified because our way of life approximates God's special plan for the age. Above all, the most troubling consequence of our theological reductions will be the propensity to live by the terrifyingly familiar axiom that the enemies of the nation are also the *enemies of God*.

W͟HO A͟RE T͟HE E͟NEMIES O͟F G͟OD? According to Saint Paul, the great apostle called to preach the gospel to the Gentiles, all of us were once enemies of God. The good news shatters all human constructions of the enemy; for the good news is that God's love is stronger than the enmity of our rebellious hearts. The good news is that Jesus Christ bore himself the judgment that we deserved by accepting the violence of the cross. "Father, forgive them; for they know not what they are doing," he said in the agony of his death, forgiving his executioners and those who mocked and reviled him (Luke 23:34). On the cross, the Son of God experienced total violence and abandonment; the particular and the universal, the historical and the cosmic, collided into salvation. A criminal's death became the unlikely place where the reconciliation between God and humanity was realized in time. "At-one-ment," the evangelical preachers sometimes say. The atoning death of Jesus Christ changes everything.

"Jesus lifted up upon the cross is drawing all men unto Himself," exclaimed the Reverend Henry Medd in a sermon entitled "The Cross: A Stumbling Block," preached in the first decade of the twentieth century.[23] The sermon was one of the great pulpit performances of a long-ago era. My copy of the sermon comes from a volume entitled *Atonement: Consisting of Sermons, Editorials, Addresses, Poems, Excerpts from Many Sources; What the Great Thinkers of This Era Have Thought and Said on This Subject,* published in 1908 in Springfield, Illinois. The "horrid scandal," the "treacherous snare," and the "stumbling block" of the cross are described as the place in the world where Jesus "consummated God's plan for the saving of humanity" in the "supreme act" of love and mercy. "The powers of hell defeating, His mighty task completing," Medd declared in the triumphant final lines. "He said that 'It is finished!'; then He sealed His work for sinful men."

Who are God's enemies? If we accept the Apostle Paul's teaching, we are all worthy to be called God's enemies, and yet because of the atoning death of Jesus, we are absolved from the judgment we deserve, freed and forgiven. "God proves his love for us in that while we were still sinners Christ died for us," Paul said in his Epistle to the Romans. "By his stripes we are healed." Not by our own stripes, or by those of our enemies, but by *his* stripes.

CHRISTIANS BELIEVE THAT TRUE knowledge of life is formed only in relationship with God. Of course, our knowledge of ourselves and the world comes from many different sources in the world. Nevertheless, we believe that the truth of ourselves and the world is fully given in the story of Jesus Christ.

In accepting Jesus Christ as Lord and Savior and being baptized into the body of Christ, Christians are brought into the love that is identical to the love of the triune God, the love perfectly shared among Father, Son, and Holy Spirit, love poured out for humanity in the gift of the Son and in the coming of the Holy Spirit. "His life, that is, His life in Himself, which is originally and properly the one and only life, leans towards this unity with our life," Karl Barth wrote in his *Church Dogmatics*.[24] "The blessings of His Godhead are so great that they overflow as blessings to us, who are not God." To be sure, for large stretches of time the reality of God's overabundant love may seem doubtful to us, dark and incomprehensible. Sometimes, too, God's mercy and love will seem to us like the very opposite of the way life appears in the real world.[25] The belief that God's love is felt, sensed, and tasted in the fellowship of the church may even seem to us an absurdity, given all we know of the church's fallibility and of our own individual failures to live faithfully, practice mercy, and seek justice. We know the church's brokenness as well as we know our own. So it goes without saying that Christians will have to learn (ever and again) what it means to say that God seeks and creates fellowship between himself and humanity, and what it means to sense, feel, and taste God's presence in the world. Yet one thing is true and true above all else: God does not exist *in* solitude or isolation but *in fellowship and in relationship with others*. In the hiddenmost mystery of God, God is perfectly giving, perfectly receiving, perfectly generous love. Love, and love overabundant—this is the basic meaning of the holiness of God. "Loving us, God does not give us something, but Himself," says Barth, "and giving us Himself, giving us His only Son, He gives us everything"[26]

"God knows our names," we used to say in the evangelical congregations. Jesus traveled into the far country of our anxious, wrecked, and violent humanity to invite all of us into the community of his love. We did not create or initiate the fellow-ship into which we have been invited; rather God invites us, as strangers, to join him in the abundant and everlasting feast. The church need never be more or less than this: belonging to one another through Jesus Christ and in Jesus Christ. Thus, we dare not speak of the community of Christ as a private association to be regulated according to our own designs. Evangelicals in the United States would do well to remember that our desire for God is not our own achievement.

Still, we cannot wait on the spontaneous activity of our born-again selves when it comes to loving God and our neighbor. Our love of God and neighbor must inspire new habits of heart and mind, habits formed by dwelling in the truth of God and speak-ing the truth. Indeed, if new habits and dispositions cannot be formed by dwelling in the truth, then what is truth? Jesus said that we are to obey the commandment to love God with all our heart and with all our soul and mind. Christians are people com-manded to love God. It matters very much how we think and speak. Christians are expected to behave differently.

Confessing and accepting Jesus Christ as Lord, we are led into a new way of seeing the world; we are given a glimpse—more than a glimpse really, though surely not yet a fully unobstructed view—of the world reconciled and redeemed. The community of Christ has been given that vision as a gift to share and to safe-guard. We fear not "those who kill the body," but the constricting of the vision, and the turning of the gift of salvation into cheap wares. There is no message greater than this: "Love not in word, neither in tongue, but in deed and in truth" and "by this we will know that we are from the truth" (1 John 3:18–19). The Christian believes that the real history of the world is revealed in the good news of Jesus Christ, and that this history overflows the boundaries of the church, for this real history moves always and everywhere toward the peaceable reign of God on earth.

The Eastern Orthodox theologian Alexander Schmemann, in his beautiful book *For the Life of the World* says that authentically Christian thought and speech is born finally of worship. A passage from this book is worth citing in full. Schmemann writes,

The Orthodox liturgy begins with the solemn doxology: "Blessed is the Kingdom of the Father, the Son and the Holy Spirit, now and ever, and unto ages of ages." From the beginning the destination is announced: the journey is to the Kingdom. This is where we are going—and not symbolically, but really. In the language of the Bible, which is *the* language of the Church, to bless the Kingdom is not simply to acclaim it. It is to declare it to be the goal, the end of all our desires and interests, of our whole life, the supreme and ultimate value of all that exists. To bless is to accept in love, and to move toward what is loved and accepted. The Church thus is the assembly, the gathering of those to whom the ultimate destination of all life has been revealed and who have accepted it. This acceptance is expressed in the solemn answer to the doxology: Amen. It is indeed one of the most important words in the world, for it expresses the agreement of the Church to follow Christ in His ascension to His Father, to make this ascension the destiny of man. It is Christ's gift to us, for only in Him can we say Amen to God, or rather He himself is our Amen to God and the Church is an Amen to Christ. Upon this Amen the fate of the human race is decided. It reveals that the movement toward God has begun. But we are still at the beginning.[27]

I like to think of prayer and worship as joining an event already in progress. We join in prayer and worship alongside all people of faith, with those who have gone from us to be with the Lord, and all those in our own towns and cities and from all parts of the world, with all who worship and pray in different places and in different languages. Whether we realize it or not—and we need to realize it!—we are more intimately connected to those with whom we share worship and prayer—rich and poor, black and white, American, Asian, African, the immigrant crossing the border, the victims of violence, the reviled, the outcast, and the pariahs, heterosexuals and homosexuals—than to partisan allies or compatriots. That might sound like a dangerous notion, but Christian discipleship is a venture filled with difficult risks and demands. The love that is perfectly lived and shared in God is the same love felt, tasted, and celebrated in the church, and because that is true, the members of the body of Christ, citizens in the kingdom of God, live according to a different standard than political loyalty and personal preferences. We must seek to live out of that difference now and always.

Are we a good and decent nation? Are we people who do justice and practice mercy? Are we people whose hearts are filled with the compassion of Christ?

In my visits to congregations around the nation, I have heard only a scattering of prayers for the slain Iraqi children and innocent civilians since the beginning of war, and I have heard these only in liberal churches. I have not heard a single prayer of sorrow, shame, or remorse in the evangelical churches. I have not heard our beloved Billy Graham beg us to pray for the victims of our bombing and killing. According to the Iraq Body Count Project, an independent human rights organization that operates the

Web site www.iraqbodycount.org, more than 55,000 civilians were killed in the first three years of fighting, with the death toll rising in the third to more than thirty-six civilian deaths per day; the killings were exceeding 600 each week by the fall of 2006.[28] In October of 2006, the British medical journal *The Lancet* announced the findings of epidemiologists, working under the sponsorship of Johns Hopkins University's Bloomberg School of Public Health, that 665,000 Iraqis had died as a result of the war.[29]

"He who does not cry out for the Jew," Dietrich Bonhoeffer once said, "may not sing Gregorian chants." Although the hour has grown late, how I wish our dear brother Billy would say, "Only he who cries out for the Iraqi child may sing 'Just As I Am.'" We must open ourselves anew to the Lord who comes to us from the far country of the triune God, which is to say, the Lord who comes to us from a country far from our own. We must sing a new song.

Chapter Six

KEEPERS OF THE MYSTERY
The Christian Tradition Speaks
(Carefully)

IF EVANGELICALS IN THE UNITED STATES, in their manner of living, have lost something of the strangeness and mystery of the faith, then the pathway to repentance and renewal includes remembering the profound ways in which historic Christianity stands far beyond our own practices and speech. Part of our journey involves regaining the freedom to speak a new and different language. I offer the following chapter as a sampling of the rich feast of wisdom given in the Christian theological tradition. Every baptized believer stands in the company of the wise teachers of the church, and, for this reason, we must turn our face back toward the origins of the faith and recall this remarkable company. The keepers of the mystery knew that life with God was the most precious gift imaginable, that respectful and reverential speech begins in silence. In contrast to the clamor of the present time and our incessant religious talk, the keepers of the faith sound a collective "hush."

In HIS NARRATIVE *The Life of Antony*, the theologian Athanasius (296–373) tells the story of a zealous young Christian who took retreat in the deserts of Syria and Egypt to live in radical obedience to Jesus. Antony became the exemplar of a generation of peculiar people journeying to the wilderness to rekindle the intensity of spiritual devotion. These barren and desert places had been the sites where the people of Israel had learned to trust in God, and now, in the fourth century after Christ, they would give rise to the earliest experiments in Christian asceticism and monastic devotion.

In the time of Moses and of Israel's release from Egypt's bondage, the desert was known as a place of revelation and awakening. In the book of Exodus, Aaron and "the whole community of Israelites" turn toward the barren land and behold the glory of Yahweh appearing in a cloud, and they then feast on the gift of sweet manna raining gloriously on the ground. There too in the wilderness, we enter the enveloping darkness of Mount Sinai upon which Yahweh descended in a pillar of fire, smoke rising as from a furnace, with blasts of trumpets and mountains trembling. There Yahweh spoke the words of the law, "Thou shalt have no other gods before me! Thou shalt . . ." In the desert Elijah took refuge for forty days and forty nights, encountering God in quietness and solitude, becoming "his own geography," "his own wild bird, with God in the center."[1] To the wilderness Jesus journeyed in preparation for ministry, and for renewal and rest, and in the desert he was tempted and assaulted by Satan, and there too where he resisted temptation and received strength for his ministry (and where he returned to renew that strength). In the desert, the pilgrim of Hebrews "went about in skins of sheep and goats . . . wandering over deserts and mountains, and in dens and caves of the earth" (Heb. 11:37–38). The Shepherd of Hermas said in the second century, "You servants of God should know that you are living in a land which is not your own. Your own city is a long way from this one."[2]

In his *Life of Antony*, Athanasius, who was Bishop of Alexandria from 328 to 373, wrote the first narrative of ascetical life in the deserts of Egypt. The Edict of Milan in 313 had brought an end to Christian persecution in the Roman Empire, and in 380 Theodosius I would make the empire a Christian state. As Christianity became the official religion, certain young believers, seeking to recover the countercultural edge of Christian devotion, left their homes in the towns and cities to live in loosely organized communes and practice their faith in the ascetic disciplines of self-renunciation and contemplative prayer. The word "asceticism" comes from the Greek *askesis*, the discipline maintained by Greek athletes in preparing their bodies for competition. In time, a movement emerged from these experiments that challenged the Christianity of the empire, giving birth eventually to the first monasteries, where ascetic discipline took ritual form, its practices codified in the Rule of Benedict and later in the Rule of Saint Francis.

The Life of Antony celebrates the devotion of a privileged young Egyptian, raised in a Christian home, who at the age of eighteen, and after the death of his parents, embarked on a pilgrimage to spiritual purity. Antony had heard a sermon on the twelfth chapter of the Gospel of Luke, "If you would be perfect, go sell what you possess and give to the poor, and you will have treasure in heaven," and immediately Antony departed and gave away his possessions. Taking instruction from a wise man in his town who had practiced the solitary life since his youth, Antony applied "all the desire and all the energy he possessed" to the pursuit of Christlikeness. Like Jesus in the wilderness, Antony encountered temptations, persecutions, and trials. He confronted great demonic forces but defied their powers.

On a walk one afternoon, Antony found an abandoned fortress teeming with reptiles in an empty place well beyond the town, and he entered the fortress and there sought to live a life of ascetic devotion. This life involved self-denial of a most extreme sort, though such ascetic vigor should surely be mistaken for weakness. In solitude and passionate devotion to Christ, Antony achieved unsurpassed clarity and strength, the "authority to tread upon serpents and scorpions," and to prevail "over all the power of the enemy." Antony learned that the demons and false-sayers flee in terror before the sign of the cross; this is what cowards do when confronted with perfect goodness. Antony further discovered that the Christian who seeks Christ will receive the power to overcome the world, and that it is therefore only through wholehearted devotion that true vision of God is found.

At the end of twenty years, Antony emerged from the fortress, remarkably unchanged in appearance, in good physical health, and sound of mind. He possessed an "utter equilibrium," the narrative says, "like one guided by reason and steadfast in that which accords with nature."[3] The sources of physical violence and warfare were confronted directly, and with spiritual weapons alone, but the spiritual weapons were sufficient. The Desert Fathers saw the Christian's struggle essentially as a metaphysical one, and they saw the desert as the theater of spiritual battle. (We should not lose sight of this point: that the tradition of Christian asceticism and martyrdom is characterized by the renunciation of physical warfare and violence.)

In his first public speech after the years in solitude, Antony reminded his fellow ascetics of the fleetingness of mortal being measured against "the ages to come." What benefit could there be in possessing worldly kingdoms and fortunes? "Why not rather own those things that we are able to take away with us—such things as prudence, justice, temperance, courage, understanding, love, concern for the poor, faith in Christ, freedom from anger, hospitality?" These are the virtues of Christian devotion, gained only in the life of "dying daily," in seeking to live every moment in full view of eternity. With God's grace, Antony remained steadfast in his faith and gained spiritual victory over the forces of Satan.

The demonology of this desert narrative will surely seem exotic to the modern mind. But even though the demons that amply populate Antony's world are primitive and exotic, they are also vaguely familiar. The demons are violent, noisy, and appear with "crashing sounds," "mass confusions," "crashing and noise and shouting." "Their ragings were fierce"; their sounds were "terrible." The demons fill the air with wild laughter and hissing, "like warriors in battle array." The demons are cunning, pretending sometimes even to be pious and righteous, reciting the Scriptures, and "arous[ing] us with prayers," incessant talk and utterances. "They pretend to speak like the devout . . . and then drag those whom they have beguiled wherever they wish."

But Antony knew that the demons did not speak the truth; their intentions were to mock the followers of Jesus, to deceive them and bring them to ruin. Victory over the demons required the soul to be purified in ascetic discipline and contemplative stillness. "The true angel of the Lord . . . had no need of hordes, nor of visible apparitions, nor of crashing sounds and rattling noises." The true Christian "wielded his authority quietly." For the "great weapon" used against the terrors of Satan was a "just life and trust in God."

The Life of Antony found wide appeal among Greek-speaking Christians in the eastern Mediterranean, as well as among Latin Christians in Gaul and Italy. Its immediate power was to attract young men and women to the life of Christian devotion at a decisive moment in the church's history.[4] The monasteries in the mountains and the desert were made into "a city by monks," who "left their own people and registered themselves for the citizenship in the heavens."[5] Although the first manual of monastic life would not be written until the Rule of St. Benedict in 530, Gregory of Nazianzus called *The Life of Antony* "a monastic rule cast in narrative." Saint Antony of Egypt and the Desert Fathers strived for spiritual authenticity in an era of compromise.[6]

Contrary to the criticism that silence, solitude, and stillness encourage indifference to the social world, the countercultural Christians of the early monastic movement understood these practices to be part of a rigorous training in the world, which produced not only heightened vision but also such Christ-shaped virtues as hospitality and neighborly love. Heightened vision and spiritual purification would lead to more loving and just social relations. "Our life and death are with our neighbor," Antony said. The ascetics lived alone, but they met in community to celebrate the Eucharist and occasionally to share table fellowship. In an especially moving passage in Athanasius's hagiography, we are given a panoramic view of the desert regions and a description of a new Christian community gathering outside the cities. We see hillsides "filled like tents with divine choirs," and "like shady groves, and like a garden by a river, and like tents which the Lord pitched, and like cedars beside the waters."[7] We see the ascetics studying, reading, fasting, and praying, and yet we also see them working for the distribution of alms, "maintaining love and harmony among themselves." "It was as if one truly looked on a land all its own— a land of devotion and righteousness," Athanasius says.[8]

How should we speak of God? The story of Saint Antony of Egypt shows us that the language of faith must be shaped by "patterning ourselves" on the way of Christ and living "in the power supplied to us by God through Jesus Christ."[9] There is no private access to God, and only those who have learned to live peaceably together in community can move safely towards solitude and quietness.[10] The theologian and Anglican priest Kenneth Leech once noted that in the writings of the Desert Fathers, "there is a repeated insistence that community and the life of sharing (Koinonia) is the life of God and of the new age, while individualism represents a regression to the unredeemed order."[11] Christian community models peace and healing for the world.[12] Saint Antony calls us back to the origins of our devotion to Christ, admonishing simplicity, obedience, and mindfulness of the language we use in seeking to keep the mystery.

IN THE SPIRITUAL AUTOBIOGRAPHY *The Confessions*, Saint Augustine (334–430) wrote of human happiness: "There is a delight which is given not to the wicked (Isaiah 48:22), but to those who worship you for no reward save the joy that you yourself are to them."[13] The "happy life" is this, Augustine said: "to set one's joy on you, grounded in you, and caused by you. That is the real thing, and there is no other."

As a child in the evangelical South, I often heard Saint Augustine's name in sermons and revivals. We pronounced it like the city in Florida, with the emphasis on the last syllable, and did not call him "Saint." Augustine was the Christian sage of the ancient church whose heart burned with a holy fire, restless until he found rest in God. Augustine gave voice to our own spiritual hunger as well, to our passion to count for eternity.

Evangelicals might do well to turn to Augustine again now, as we survey the wreckage of our careless talk and diminished passion. Augustine confronts us with the mystery of existence and the fragility of language. When we speak of God, we speak at once of perfect goodness and rest, the glow of being that illuminates every horizon, the source of life. "You called and cried out loud and shattered my deafness. You were radiant and resplendent, you put to flight my blindness. You were fragrant, and I drew in my breath and now pant after you. I tasted you, and I feel but hunger and thirst for you. You touched me, and I am set on fire to attain the peace which is yours." God is the Good in need of no other good, perfect rest, the still point of every center. For you, O Lord, creator of all being, "you yourself are your own rest."[14]

In the *Confessions*, the entire span of life is portrayed as a theater of the listening God. God listens, and God hears. There is no place, however hostile, intimate, or seemingly bereft of grace, that is beyond the range of God's hearing. All our words, self-examinations, defenses, and petitions are embraced by the listening God, who hears and heals like a wise counselor. God in turn invites us to a time of listening, into a listening silence. *The Confessions* is an exercise in holy listening.

The Catholic theologian Romano Guardini once said that Augustine writes out of "amazement over existence."[15] He is amazed by the realization that all existence springs originally (intimately and ecstatically) from the word of God, which transcends time as it enables time. The word is spoken eternally in Christ. All objects and events, all words and meanings, are instruments of that divine word. As Augustine says, "Thus, O God, I should be nothing, utterly nothing, unless you were in me—or rather unless I were in You, *of whom and by whom and in whom are all things. So it is, Lord, so it is.*"[16] Interestingly, even the exercise of reading becomes a lesson in longing, for in order to get to the next word in a sentence, one must let go of the word preceding it. Meanings unfold like sunbursts of understanding and illumination, forming the reader and the page, only to fade into the past, into memory and forgetting. Longing moves forward in search of the fuller meaning. Only God's hearing, and thus only God's word, endures the fleeting exchanges of our mortal lives. The word of God endures forever.

Augustine's interior conversation of his journey with God must be read in light of the significant fact that he had recently been made a bishop. As the head of the church in Hippo, Augustine would lead an even more active life than he had as a priest. The *Confessions* are not then a summons to inwardness or quietism, but a testimony to the brilliance, limits, and fragility of language, the preciousness of language felt even more intensely amidst interruption and distraction. In the autobiography, Augustine seems at times overwhelmed by the mystery of the word, and his writing becomes a kind of interrogation of the divine being. "Who are you, radiant and resplendent Lord and God, you who cannot be squeezed into categories of thought or human designs?"[17] "Are there in You parts greater and smaller? Or are You not in every place at once in the totality of Your being, while yet nothing contains You?" At times, as Father Guardini observes, the writing seems fraught with tension, as the saint of the church seeks to render in language the "feeling of uncertain suspension," the "groping for a hold," the bracing apprehension of God's goodness (Guardini's words).[18] How do I exist? Who am I? How is it that I can even ask this question? Questions pile on to questions. If I am suspended in time, what might I be suspended from? Is that suspension God?

Augustine's answers emerge out of self-analysis, but they are not self-referential. The answers point always beyond themselves toward the Good which is God, the Good in need of no other good, the God who is perfect stillness and rest, the source of all things. "Anyone who claims for his own property what you offer for all to enjoy, and wishes to have exclusive rights to what belongs to everyone, is driven from the common truth to his own private ideas, that is from truth to a lie."[19] God's claim is total but not totalitarian. It is total because truth cannot be served half-heartedly, divided among friends and devoured in easy spoonfuls. The truth of God takes time to taste, feel, and know. It may lead down a long and circuitous road of probing introspection, but truth is worth the sacrifice.

This is the paradox so alien to the modern view: God's truth is all-consuming but not enslaving. It is the light that shines through the world's darkness and reveals its real meanings in obedience, love, and worship: "You are great, Lord, and highly to be praised (Ps. 47:2): great is your power and your wisdom is immeasurable (Ps. 146:5)." Humankind is but a little piece of God's creation, made in God's image, gifted with the desire to praise God (2 Cor. 4:10), even as we carry within us the witness of sin and mortality. To praise God is to take pleasure in praising

God, because, as Augustine says, "you have made us for your-self, and our heart is restless until it finds its rest in you."[20] Truth sets the heart free to live in peace with the Creator and creation. Truth awakens life.

Augustine teaches us urgently needed lessons on the beauty and brilliance of language, about the majesty of the word and the gift of life. Christian existence is meant as a testimony of the word. For the word of God is the condition of all that we do and say. God spoke, and the word of God created the heavens and earth. This means that if Christians are to become people of truth, then we must be marked as disciples of Jesus Christ by our respect for the word and by the passion to speak the truth in love. "All things come into being through him." Christians must learn to live as participants in this gift.

GOD "IS NOT A SPECTER OR PHANTASM to be transformed accord-ing to anyone's whim," wrote the Protestant reformer John Calvin (1509–1564) in his great work *Institutes of the Christian Reli-gion.*[21] For Calvin, genuine piety begins with the reverence de-serving the "one and only God." God is fully righteous and just, the author of perfect peace, and until we measure our own efforts in relation to that greater righteousness, we will never truly know ourselves. Calvin wanted to restore to the everyday flow of Chris-tian life a living, palpable sense of God's mystery, majesty, and holiness, and he believed that a sober understanding of the rela-tionship between the righteous God and our rebellious nature was the necessary first step in an honest self-appraisal. If we wish to honor the one and only God, we should remember that we dare not "pluck away even a particle of his glory" and that God must retain what is fully God's own. Calvin says, "Whenever any observances of piety are transferred to some one other than the true God, sacrilege occurs."

The worship of false gods is as old as human history. As Calvin tells the story, there was once a time when human superstition inspired divine honors for the sun, the stars, the seasons, and natural forces. Then there was a time when ambition adorned mortals with the "spoils of God," profaning everything sacred by transferring it to the human frame. Although there remained in our consciousness "the principle of worshiping a supreme Being," it was nonetheless a common custom "to offer sacrifices indiscriminately to tutelary divinities, lesser gods, or dead heroes." Humanity fell repeatedly into the error of distributing among "a great throng" those qualities and attributes which God "rigorously deserves for himself alone." We fashioned idols out of finite loyalties.

What must we then do to know and honor the one true God? Calvin says we must have the humility to realize that we stand and are upheld by God alone, that "naked and empty-handed," we "flee to his mercy, repose entirely in it, hide deep within it, and seize upon it alone for righteousness and merit." In Jesus Christ, God's face shines in perfect grace and gentleness, even upon those who profane his name, betray his trust, and dishonor our baptism. Thus, as Calvin teaches us, it is to Christ we flee, silent and waiting. For in Christ God's mercy is revealed to "all who seek and wait upon it with faith." There, in the place of God's amazing grace, we relinquish our will to control others, and we begin to rehearse a new moral law; "to love those who hate us, to repay their evil deeds with benefits, to return blessings for reproaches." Beholding the glory of God, refracted through human sin and brokenness, resplendent in divine revelation, we are able to see the sparks of divinity in all things; the world appears in a new light, and the image of God radiates throughout creation, as both friends and enemies are seen against the horizon of grace. The never-ending love of God "cancels and effaces" our transgressions, and "with its beauty and dignity allures us to love and embrace" all people. We are all sinners, to be sure, but those who behold the divine radiance speak with the tremor of astonishment. They do not linger over depravity.

"We ought not to think that the Godhead is like unto gold, or silver, or stone, graven by art and device of man," Calvin wrote in the *Institutes*. There might have once been a time in the history of salvation when God overlooked the ignorance of the idolater, but now, under the radiance of the resurrected Christ, "he commandeth men that they should all everywhere repent," "*grasping Christ's righteousness.*" Calvin reminds us of the fundamental affirmation that only God is God, and that there is a fear proper to genuine piety. This is not the fear that turns us back from the world or wraps itself in numbing platitudes; not the fear that drowns us in shame or paralyzes thought; proper fear is that born of reverence and humility. God is not in the business of filling the gap between our private desires and our public rewards. In encountering the living God, we encounter the one who comes to us from a foreign country speaking a new language, singing a new song, and the living God of Jesus Christ will not be mocked.

It was not until a few days after the death of Blaise Pascal (1623–1662) that a helper in his Paris home discovered in the lining of the deceased's doublet a folded parchment that included the following words:

FIRE!

God of Abraham, God of Isaac, God of Jacob, not of the
philosophers and scholars.

Certitude. Certitude. Feeling. Joy. Peace.

God of Jesus Christ.

Deum meum et Deum vestrum.

Thy faithfulness of the world and of everything, except
God.

He is to be found only by the ways taught in the
Gospel.

For eight years Pascal took care to sew the document in the lining of his coat, each time he obtained a new one.[22]

In Pascal's words, "FIRE" was the most appropriate metaphor for the experience of God. Fire is both a consuming mystery and an illuminating power. Encounter with God for God's sake would be an encounter that transformed the world from the inside out. "He shall baptize you with the Holy Spirit and with fire," John the Baptist proclaimed of the coming Messiah. At Pentecost, the day of shimmering ecstasy described in the Acts of the Apostles, the Spirit came in "a sound from heaven as of a rushing mighty wind," and all the houses were filled with the sound, and there appeared to all the people "cloven tongues like as of fire," which "sat upon each of them," as the King James Version reads. The FIRE encountered by Pascal was the "consuming fire" of God, the flaming bush that burns but never burns out.[23]

Pascal writes:

> Joy, joy, joy, tears of joy . . .
> Let me not be separated from Him eternally.
> "This is the eternal life, that they might know Thee,
> the only true God, and the one whom Thou has sent,
> Jesus Christ."

What does it mean to speak of the holiness of God? Reverence and joy distinguish our approach to God as one marked off and withdrawn from frivolous use.[24] That the God of Abraham and Isaac—the God marked off and yet alive with history—revealed himself in Jesus Christ, as Christians believe, does not give Christians license to presume that the limits on God's holiness have been removed (although one might conclude from the rhetoric of American Christendom that an exemption has been made that permits us to inspect holiness as if it were a useful commodity). The God who revealed himself in Jesus Christ is the God beyond god, whose name can never be contained in our finite systems of thought and control. And it is only by accepting this fact—the chastening freedom of God from our desperate attempts to domesticate and colonize transcendence—that the ecstasies of the Spirit are unleashed in our lives: "Joy, joy, joy, tears of joy."

Pascal reminds contemporary Christians—especially we who have taken great efforts to make the world acceptable to our needs—that a certain suspicion of the world remains a necessary disposition. For human experience and all its dimensions, including—some might say especially—religion, are tainted with an original corruption. "Men never do evil so completely and cheerfully as when they do it from religious conviction," he says in the *Pensées*.[25] Pascal's meditations unsettle every effort to identify our wills with God's.

To be sure, it may embarrass us to read Pascal's fussy remarks on theater and popular entertainment, especially those of us in the evangelical churches who have worked so hard to gain respectability from our cultured friends and associates, who have come to assume that the delights of the world can be easily enough baptized. But we might learn from our current political idolatries that it is time to hold up our amusements and judgments to the light of pure goodness. "So we depart from the theatre with our heart so filled with all the beauty and tenderness of love, the soul and the mind so persuaded of its innocence, that we are quite ready to receive its first impressions."[26] We have cast off so many of our old inhibitions that we are no longer able to appreciate the difference between first impressions and eternal verities.

In this manner, Pascal's famous axiom on stillness, "I have concluded that the whole misfortune of men comes from a single thing, and that is their inability to sit quietly in a room," is about a spiritual disposition that nurtures a healthy suspicion. It is about the suspicion that distinguishes the demands in the world that are born of self-glorification from those born of the desire to bring glory to God. "It is not enough that a thing be beautiful," Pascal says, "it must be suitable to the subject." In other words, much that we praise and adore remains untouched by the urgent question, namely, whether that object, commitment, or value is suitable to those who bear witness to the Prince of Peace.

Thomas Merton said in a letter to Argentinian writer Victoria Ocampo, "[There] might be too much bitterness and pessimism in Pascal's solitude and yet he is so right and so acute."[27] However learned, however cosmopolitan, however politically aware and culturally engaged he or she may become, the Christian must always register a clear and final deferral on the world's favor in view of the cross and its benefits. World-weariness can surely become its own form of self-righteousness (and an unbearable form at that), but taking stock of human sinfulness in the shadow of God's righteousness is Pascal's great correction, and one which might at least discourage such confident notions as that of angels riding in the storm of our military invasion of Iraq.[28]

In HER SHORT, brilliant life, Saint Thérèse of Lisieux (1873–1897) learned that the meaning of Christian devotion is found in ordinary splendor, in attunement to a deeper mundane, which she called "the little way."

"Jesus does not demand great deeds," Thérèse wrote. "All He wants is self-surrender and gratitude . . . He needs nothing from us except our love."[29] Saint Thérèse amends the wisdom of the Christian Distinction—that God would be perfectly God without creating the world—with a plea for greater complexity: God seeks our love in a way analogous to romantic desire. God is love ecstatically reaching out for contact, and thus God desires our love as the fulfillment of the drama of redemption. God does not need our love in order to be more fully God. Rather, God desires our love that we might more fully know him and that we might be more fully human—and that is all we need.

How dramatically Saint Thérèse 's little way contrasts with the road of enormous schemes and colossal ambitions. The latter may lead to self-expansion and personal power. It may produce dazzling results and influence millions. But it should not be confused with the path that leads to intimacy with God. This way is not the way of Jesus.

Saint Thérèse was drawn to the passage in the Song of Songs, the poem of sensual love in the Hebrew Bible, where the poet says to his beloved, "Draw me in your footsteps, let us run" (1:4 NJB). She found sufficiency in selfless devotion and its fairly untested illuminations and energies. "I ask Jesus to draw me into the flames of his love and to unite me so closely to him that he lives and acts in me," she wrote. "I feel that the more the fire of love encompasses my heart, the more I shall say: 'Draw me,' and the more will those who are near to mine 'run swiftly in the sweet odour of the Beloved.'"[30] Thus, she understood that it is not force and will that move the world toward God, but "the fire of love" and the "lever" of prayer. Love and prayer enable "those still battling in the world" to move the world closer to God and to "go on moving it till the end of time."[31]

Thérèse of Lisieux, like all the saints, speaks to our situation with gentleness but with urgency. The stories of the church's great lovers reveal, as the theologian Henri de Lubac writes, "a new life, a new sphere of existence, with unsuspected depths— but also with a resonance hitherto unknown to us and now at last revealed."[32] The great lovers remind us that the resurrection does not remove the wounds of the cross. As Augustine said, the wounds of the church still bleed in the sufferings of the faithful.[33] These men and women remind us that our own righteousness is far from the mark of God's own and that we cannot simply appeal to our fallenness as an excuse for our willful distortion of the faith. The saints show us that the Christian tradition impresses upon us the humility to listen and learn. The church should be like a beggar, constantly begging for forgiveness, a mendicant church making lament in the world for the world's sins, and for our own.[34] True saintliness is found in straightforwardness and simplicity.

K ARL BARTH (1886–1968) DELIVERED THE ADDRESS "The Righteousness of God" in the Town Church of Aarau, Switzerland, in January of 1916. The address, published in his extraordinary book *The Word of God and the Word of Man*, is an attack on bourgeois religion as powerful and passionate as any other in the history of the Christian tradition. In a world at war, with the past century's hopes of enlightened self-expansion chastened if not devastated, Barth exposed the theological mistake at the heart of the political crisis of his time.

Barth's concern in the essay is the future of the Christian faith in the wake of its complicity in war and nationalism. After accommodating the gospel to the ambitions of the nation, can Christians ever learn to behold the living God who in revealing himself in Jesus Christ shakes the foundations of human culture? Barth asks how it might be possible to experience God's presence amidst the ruins of the church's mistaken loyalty, and he asks that we begin again with Saint John the Baptist's glorious proclamation in the Gospel of Matthew: "Prepare ye the way of the Lord. Make straight in the desert a highway for our God. Every valley shall be exalted, and every mountain and hill shall be made low; and the crooked shall be made straight, and the rough places plain: and the glory of the LORD shall be revealed!" (Isa. 40:3–5 KJV).

Every day we have before our eyes the consequences of human rebellion: "disquiet, disorder, and distress in forms minute and

gross, obscure and evident."[35] Our uneasy conscience may sometimes stir in us an anxious mindfulness of that greater righteousness, but human conscience cannot do more than point into
the distance. It can make us aware of a greater righteousness by
speaking of the will that remains true to itself, a will that eludes
our desperate attempts to fashion comfortable gods. But conscience cannot reveal the living God. Barth says that the first step
is to accept the folly of our religious constructions and ideals.
This is where the good news comes in: Into the midst of our great
apprehension, beyond our "warped and weakened will," as irresistible and unbroken as the theme of a Bach fugue, the Bible
proclaims that there is another will that is "straight and pure,"
and which, "when it once prevails, must have other, wholly other,
issues than these we see today"—war, violence, greed, famine.
There is a will of God that is pure and righteous.

In view of the good news, the question then is whether we are
prepared to accept this will and all that it brings, a "radical overturn of life." But this radical overturn is our only hope. Nothing
short of a complete shift in perspective can save us when we are
left alone to fend with the devastating consequences of our idolatry. Most of us are not prepared to change our lives. We live in
fear of change. We recoil before the radical overturn and, in our
fear and panic, we try to build havens to preserve our cherished
values and to protect ourselves from the righteousness of God.

We build havens of morality, construct them out of thrift, family, patriotism, and vocation; and we convince ourselves that our
customs, traditions, and values are the foundations of true justice. *We build a haven of the state and the law.* But the righteousness of the state, while it may bring order to our lives and
accomplish noble ends, fails finally "to touch the inner character

of the world-will." The state and the law may protect us from our enemies, and from our own worst habits (although it may fail at this too), but the state and the law will never be able to prepare the way of the Lord. *We build havens of religion.* In fear of the righteousness of God, we turn to religion for a "wonderful sense of safety and security." We might be alarmed by the stirring of an uneasy conscience and by the guilt that we have domesticated transcendence, but in our religious zeal "we have gone no further than to play sleepily with shadow pictures of the divine righteousness." The pointing hand of John the Baptist has lost its strangeness.[36] We stick ourselves into the world as gods and goddesses. "Religious arrogance permits itself simply everything," Barth would later say.[37]

And it also serves a desperate purpose. These havens give us a "wonderful sense of safety and security," a "pleasant green island" of serenity amidst the uncertainties of history. But the havens have become our prisons. In our retreat to morality, law, and religion, we forget the difference between our finite longings and the God who comes to us anew in the miracle of Jesus Christ. The God we trust, the God toward whom we turn to sanctify our values and preferences and to find warrant for our campaigns and to affirm our way of life—this God *is* dead. This God *is* a fantasy, a wishful projection, an irrational defense against fear and uncertainty. Thus, Barth says, it is "high time for us to confess freely and gladly," that "this god, to whom we have built the tower of Babel, is not God."[38]

Barth sounds like one of the great prophets of modern atheism in sounding this note, especially the philosopher Friedrich Nietzsche, in his assault on Christendom.[39] "Hearing that the old god is dead," Nietzsche had written, "we feel ourselves illumined as by a new dawn . . . the whole expanse of the sea, our sea, is accessible to us once more. Never before, perhaps, was there such an open sea." But Barth sees beyond the nihilist turn—beyond unlimited self-creation and pure autonomy—to the living God encountered anew, the God beyond god. Barth sees the empty tomb. On Easter morning, "God himself, the real, the living God" appears in glory and grace.[40]

Still, we wonder how amidst the chaos of our time we might experience the risen Christ in glory and grace. Barth, the pastor, labor organizer, anti-Nazi intellectual, and dissident theologian, startles us in his response: "By being still!" he says. "By learning to listen." But being still and learning to listen do not bring action to a halt; stillness and listening lead us away from the familiar and to places in the world—and in the self—where the word of God can be heard: to desert places, to the wildernesses, to forgotten and excluded spaces. We are led to desolate regions and to far away fields where we can remember that God's will is "not a continuation of our own." Barth says we must learn to be silent, for in silence "true redemption" begins. Our hope is found "not [in] noise but quiet." Thus, we must begin again with God by returning to the origins, to the scandal of the cross and the miracle of grace. We must learn to live, think, act and speak in light of the inescapable axiom that only God is God. "Thou shalt have no other gods before me."

This will not be easy. Beginning again with God is "a task beside which all cultural, moral, and patriotic duties, all efforts in 'applied religion,' are child's play." In the humility of stillness and quiet, we give ourselves over to God.

Barth concludes this 1916 address from Aarau:

> To do his will . . . means to begin with him anew. His will is not a corrected continuation of our own. It approaches ours as a Wholly Other. There is nothing for our will except a basic re-creation. Not a reformation but a re-creation and re-growth.
>
> [In] place of despair a childlike joyfulness will come; a joy that God is so much greater than we thought. Joy that his righteousness has far more depth and meaning than we had allowed ourselves to dream. Joy that from God much more is to be expected for our poor, perplexed, and burdened life than with our idealism, our principles, and our Christianity. . . . So much more to be expected!
>
> *Have* we joy enough? Are the springs which might be flowing really flowing so abundantly? Have we barely yet begun to feel the true creative joy of God's presence?[41]

It remains to be seen whether the rumbling beneath the tower of Babel that we are beginning to now experience in the United States will be strong enough to bring us nearer to this creative joy and restored vision. Perhaps the narcosis of faith-based ambition cannot be resisted by the churches. Perhaps we really are addicted to the sound of our voice. But God will not be mocked, and as Barth concluded in his talk (ever the fierce Calvinist), "Opportunity offers. We may take the new way. Or we may not. Sooner or later we shall. There is no other."[42]

FINALLY, IN HIS BRIEF ESSAY ENTITLED "The End of Time Is the Time of No Room," the Catholic monk, theologian, and writer

Thomas Merton (1915–1968) pondered the meaning of the Advent story. In particular, he asked about the often neglected fact that the "pure peace, pure joy" of the Messiah entered history in a manger because there was no room for him in the inn (Luke 2:7). What does it mean to preach the gospel in a world so inhospitable to the Prince of Peace? Merton says we must first understand the severity of our present age.

The time of the end is a time of hostility to God's peace; it is "the time of massed armies," "wars and rumors of war," the time of huge crowds moving over the earth, of "men withering away from fear, of flaming cities and sinking fleets, of smoking lands laid waste, of technicians planning grandiose acts of destruction."[43] The time of the end is the "time of the Crowd," of "suspicion, hatred and distrust." The Messiah was born into a world that offers no room to the peace that passes all understanding, a world that assaults innocence and purity, a world which comes so easily undone in seeking frantically to shield itself from the new light of the God born in a lowly manger. Hearing the gospel message now, we respond with an arsenal of efficient means, with displacement and evasion, in an intensification of noise and aggression, in relentless flight and movement, and by all manner of techniques that compress and suffocate space. The gospel is "spoken to a world, where precisely because of 'the vast indefinite roar of armies on the move and the restlessness of turbulent mobs,' the Good News can be heard only with difficulty."

In the flow of our American days, there is too much news, too much information, too much talk. The result, Merton says, is that there is little room left for the good news, the story that reveals the meaning of all other stories. The barrage of data has become for us a "new noise in the mind," a way of drowning out the quietness

that might otherwise re-center our lives on truth. Ways of escape
and paths to authenticity prove infuriatingly difficult to find; everything eventually "blends into the same monotonous and meaning-
less rumor." Searching in vain for quiet spaces within and without,
our lives are shaped by a thematics of escape, and there is only
flight and movement and a semblance of repose.

What then happens in this time of compressing space to the
"Great Joy," the word announced to shepherds living in the fields
and in the countryside? Is that miraculous report not overwhelmed by the vast and clamorous march of annihilating forces:
"marshaled, numbered, marched here and there, taxed, drilled,
armed, worked to the point of insensibility, dazed by information,
drugged by entertainment, surfeited with everything, nauseated
with the human race and with ourselves, nauseated with life"?
The barrage of images wears down the soul, humiliates the word,
and abandons us to transience. "As the end approaches," writes
Merton, "there is no room for quiet. There is no room for solitude. There is no room for thought. There is no room for attention,
for the awareness of our state." How can we make time again for
being simply Christian?

Merton points us back to the origins of our faith—to a vision of
Christ living quietly among those who can find no room in the inn,
among those who are "rejected by power because they are regarded as weak, those who are discredited, who are denied the status of persons, tortured, exterminated." The Christ of the gospel
declares to the gods of the "armies, the missiles, the weapons, the
bombs," that they are but demons. Jesus defeats the warrior Mars
on the cross and makes his own body the place where everlasting
peace explodes into time and history. The gospel confronts us with
our origins: the story of the God born in a manger because there

was no room for him in the inn; the story of the Messiah slain for the sins of the world; the beloved community of "desert-dwellers, wilderness wanderers, and nomads" living in resistance to the benumbing transactions and flattening exchanges of "the time of no room." Being simply Christian means being one who lives in anticipation of the "eschatological convocation," being re-formed by "Evangelical Joy."[44]

The real history of the world comes to us in the story of a stranger. We can distort that history with lies and deceptions, or we can seek to make our world a place where that history is seen and experienced. Merton invites us into the quiet and affirming goodness of the Christmas gospel, where "the special and heavenly light . . . shines around the coming of the Word into the world," into the miraculous story of life's victory over death, which is this Evangelical Joy, proclaimed in gladness and received in gratitude.

WHAT CAN WE IN THE AMERICAN CHURCH learn from Brother Merton and these keepers of the mystery? First and foremost, we can learn that it is not through our ambitions and agendas that we are drawn into the love of God, but through simplicity spirited with fervor. The triumph of the image, the angle, and the talking points is tearing apart the mystery of God's word, as well as in a more ordinary sense, the spoken and written word. Christians must accept responsibility for preparing the conditions in which God's voice can be heard again in glory and in truth. The only way to move forward now is by looking backward and remembering who we are and whence we came.

Do we stop speaking of God? Should our worship and devotion

be carried out in silence? The opposite of holy silence is not words but noise.[45] Antony of Egypt teaches us that beyond the clamor of the false gods lies not the absence of language but silence spilling into thoughtful speech. It is difficult to hear the true word amidst all the noise, and for this reason we must ourselves become keepers of the mystery and dwell a while in the stillness of God. We cannot remain silent forever. We must be rather like Mary Magdalene and "that other Mary" who left the empty tomb "with fear and great joy," and went out to bring the disciples word (Matt. 28:8).

Chapter Seven

LEARNING TO BE QUIET IN A NOISY NATION (AND IN A NATION OF NOISY BELIEVERS)

WRITING A HALF-CENTURY AGO, the Protestant theologian Paul Tillich made a recommendation, half in jest, that the church impose a thirty-year moratorium on all its "archetypal language."[1] Tillich, a liberal German observer of American Christian culture, was struck by the tendency of religious people to drag God into every conversation without concern for the attendant theological casualties. Tillich claimed that the manner of religious speech observed in popular Christianity was but a crude form of self-flattery, and we should thus enter into a time of religious silence in hopes that a "new terminology" might someday arise.

In his writings from prison, the German theologian and pastor Dietrich Bonhoeffer also admonished Christians to silence, but his admonition had about it a spirit of repentance and lament. Bonhoeffer thought that Christians living in the ruins of the church's political captivity should commit themselves to the "arcane discipline," an ancient and nearly forgotten practice of the church whose purpose is to preserve the mysteries of the faith, to guard sacred language against desecration, and to limit its use to devotional and liturgical practices. Until that day when Christians are able to speak a "new language," a day that will be "liberating and redeeming," the "Christian cause will be a silent and hidden affair." As Bonhoeffer wrote in prison, "a secret discipline must be restored whereby the *mysteries* of the Christian faith are protected against profanation."[2] The practice of the arcane discipline, he imagined, would also accompany a period of sweeping ecclesial reforms. The church would give away all its assets and serve the world anonymously, refusing to call attention to itself. "All Christian thinking, speaking and organizing" shall be limited to "prayer and righteous action." This is the only appropriate language for a church in ruins. "The time of words is over," he said.

Rowan Williams, the Archbishop of Canterbury, in a sermon preached during the 2006 Berlin Centenary Celebration of Bonhoeffer's birth, remarked that being a Christian means "to believe that we are commanded and authorized to say certain things to the world; to say things that will make disciples of all nations."[3] Christians remain ever mindful of how they speak when they confess the beliefs they hold. "Our words matter," Williams said. "We have to think with care about them and to try and know something of how they will be heard." Words matter indeed. We can speak in a manner that opens the world to the peace of God and helps release people from captivity, or we can speak in way that creates the opposite effect and block channels of grace. When we become mindful of our destructive use of language, we must then take time to be silent, and in silence, be still, pray, and think.

Teaching about christ begins in silence," Bonhoeffer told
the students in his 1933 lectures on the doctrine of Christ. "The
silence of the church is the silence before the Word."[4] These lectures were delivered in Berlin only months before Bonhoeffer left
his academic post for pastoral work and opposition to the nazified church. The lectures were published posthumously, collected
mainly from student notes, under the title *Christ the Center*. At
times, they appear uneven and exceedingly ponderous. Nonetheless, the total effect of the lectures is to offer vigorous and unequivocal testimony to Jesus Christ as the mediator of all reality.
The man or woman in Christ lives in reference to a new center.
Christian faith does not begin with abstract concepts such as *lo-
gos* or "Being," nor is it based on tribal loyalties or local traditions. Christian thinking and acting emerge from an encounter
with Jesus Christ, which brings the crusading ego to stillness before the word.

In contrast to the German church and its elites, who had
worked hard to recast the Christian faith in terms compatible with
the racist ideals of National Socialism, Bonhoeffer claimed that
authentic Christianity would need to be marked first and foremost
by the affirmation of Jesus Christ as Lord over all creation—over
all rulers, principalities, and powers—and thus as the hidden and
cosmic center of reality. "The meaning of history is tied up with
an event which takes place in the depth and hiddenness of a man
who ended on the cross," Bonhoeffer said. "The meaning of history is found in the humiliated Christ."[5] The cross chastens our
attempts to replace or to amplify the crucified Christ with the
folksy charms of the beguiling politician and the triumphalistic
regime—"with messianic expectations of history." Jesus Christ,

the encountering word of God, who meets us in the strangeness of the gospel (and in the stranger, outcast and oppressed), cannot be assimilated into the existing order, however much we may try. "In so far as the Church proclaims the Word," Bonhoeffer says, "it falls down silently in truth before the inexpressible."

What then should Christians do in the ruins of compromise and accommodation? To speak of Jesus Christ means, first of all, to approach God in silence. Only when the church speaks out of holy silence and the deepest reverence can Jesus Christ be proclaimed in truth and power.

"You are fed up with words," Thomas Merton wrote, two decades after Bonhoeffer's death, "and I don't blame you. I am nauseated by them sometimes. I am also, to tell the truth, nauseated by ideals and with causes. This sounds like heresy, but I think you will understand what I mean."[6] It doesn't sound like heresy to me. It sounds like water flowing out of parched ground.

"Be still and know that I am God," the psalmist says (46:10). Be still and *know*. This passage takes us up short; but it is not an invitation to passivity or quietism. The psalm rather offers an invitation to learn again who we are as children of the living God, to dwell in thanksgiving for God's love, to stand in worshiping stillness in God's presence, to behold God's resplendent beauty and alien peace, putting aside the relentless production of programs and projects and our grand self-estimations, and to abide in Evangelical Joy.

Evangelicals are often driven by a messianic impulse. If there is a legitimate fear of our influence on political leaders, it is this presumption to be acting in the world with divine authority. We storm onto the scene to save the day. Our domain is a fully sufficient order of righteousness, and the unilateral prerogative of power and certitude is the engine that keeps our cause alive. We are folks on a mission.

Still, our messianic impulse rests on a weak notion of the historic Christian faith. One might even say that we deny the efficacy of Christ's atoning death on the cross by acting as if our own heroic efforts complete the work of salvation. Instead of finding the grace to live in simple devotion to Jesus, we replace his redemptive death with our fabulous and elaborate plans. We become the vice-regents of God.

The noisiness of our religion may be part and parcel of our messianic impulse, but it is also, I think, a sign that we are frightened of the silences of God. We enslave ourselves to a pace that makes it difficult to notice how far we have actually moved away from simplicity and love. The Swiss-German philosopher Max Picard wrote in his meditations on solitude, "In the modern world the individual no longer faces silence, no longer faces the community, but faces only the universal noise."[7] Yet we prefer the noise. The noise feels comforting; the ubiquitous drone protects us from ourselves and from God.

Each one of us, and each of our children, is confronted with oppressive expectations and demands. As much as I may recoil from the image of the "Superkid," sociologist David Elkind's description of the one "who has spectacular powers and competence even as an infant," I am complicit as a parent in the hypermanagement of childhood.[8] My sons' little leagues played twenty-four six-inning games with more than twenty-five practices scheduled between March and May, including the week of their spring break. At the same time, their teachers assign hours of homework after having them in school all day—and this on top of music lessons, sports practice, chores at home, church groups, Young Life, Wyldlife, and all the other things that need to be accomplished. Everyone lays claim to our children—coaches, youth workers, music leaders, advertisers, gun companies, Army recruiters, advertisers. And parents are too often willing accomplices. Most of us are so busy attending to our own demands as mothers and fathers, sifting through the ever-expanding field of duties, obligations, and loyalties, that we have precious few resources with which to protest the intrusions.

The situation feels hopeless. The helping hand of e-mail technology in the work week may save us time in a brief written response when in the past a phone call or conversation would have been required, but it also encourages an exaggerated sense of accessibility, which is inevitably mocked by an even more relentless flow of words, images, and verbal nonsense (so much of my spam mail is letters and symbols thrown randomly on a page).

A brief digression: About six years ago, before my family's move to Virginia, I was downloading documents onto floppy disks in my office, when it came to my attention that I was in possession of two e-mail accounts, and that the e-mail address for me appearing on the official college Web site—on a faculty list I had never noticed—was not the same address or account I had been using for the past three years, the one printed on my professional cards and stationery. I accessed the other account as quickly as I could and received the alarming news, "You have 475 new messages!" (These were the days before the junk mail plague.) I scrolled through the messages, through the months and years of unanswered letters, through speaking invitations, pleas for term paper extensions, queries from colleagues around the nation and world, requests for recommendation letters, notes from old friends hoping to reconnect at an upcoming conference, and mountains of official notifications from college administrators. But what intrigued me more than the discovery of my mysterious account was that all of these letters—with only about a half dozen exceptions—had eventually been resolved without my response. At least, this seemed safe to assume as several of the more recent messages started off with something like, "Charles, don't worry about getting back to me about _____ I called _____ and he/she answered my question/wrote the letter/is filling in for me/can moderate the session/said you never answered anyway."

I did not come of age in the Internet generation. I came of age getting letters in stamped envelopes, which I would put in a drawer and read in good time. There is no doubt in my mind that life was better then. Our written correspondence stood on its own merit and didn't need a "prompt response" and a flurry of clarifications and action-items to certify its legitimacy.

In any case, it feels to me that the time we now save creates new and more complicated demands. In the end, I forget how to be quiet because I have made decisions in favor of diversions and duties with an inflated sense of my relational capabilities. And as much as I may long for simplicity and straightforwardness, it feels easier, and vaguely flattering, to submit to the duties and diversions than to sit quietly in a room with my child, sharing stories or admiring the afternoon sky.

Similarly, I think many Christians in the United States, white Christians in particular, have not been able to trust in God with all our hearts and thus to follow freely the way of the cross.[9] We are terrified of a moment when we might be left risking everything on the truth of God. Instead, we fight battles intended to secure our worldly and political importance, and we shield ourselves from God's promise to bless, to sustain, to nurture, and to suffice.

How can we regain faith's authenticity? I propose that we join the keepers of the mystery in a season of silence and together pray for deliverance and renewal. When we were strangers to the household of God, God invited us inside; how much more can we expect as friends. This is very good news: We are accepted in our tragic-comic creatureliness and freed from our messianic ambition to act like gods in the world. The Protestant Reformers spoke of the "prevenience of grace": God reaching out to us in love before we ever thought of reaching out to him. Grace is the miracle of love washing over our arrogance and rebellion. Grace means we are relieved of the burden of being the vice-regents of God; we are asked simply to abide with Christ in the Garden of Gethsemane. This is also what it means to be human. The realization that I am not God—and that it is destructive of myself, others, and creation when I try to be God—gives me room to be the person God created me to be. Think about it: amazing grace poured out for all humanity in Jesus, freely, lovingly given to us all, undeserved, undeserving. Or better, hum the sweet old song softly, begin to feel the gentle abundance of it all, the weight and beauty of everlasting love.

Grace brings our fawning theatrical piety to an appropriate end, for God has done for us what we could not do for ourselves— and what we should not try to do. Grace opens us to God and to life. There is therefore no condemnation for those who are in Jesus Christ, nor is there need to prove our righteousness through heroic and world-transformative activity. In doing for us what we could never do ourselves, God says, *be still and know that I am God;* in waiting you will find strength and courage. The manic, crusading desire to manage the script comes to rest in the quiet and free spaces of Evangelical Joy. "Likewise the Spirit helps us in our weakness; for we do not know how to pray as we ought, but that very Spirit intercedes with sighs too deep for words" (Rom. 8:26).

Being still will not be easy. We live in movement and flight. We network, multi-task, micro-manage, and orchestrate. Pascal was right: We are people who crave "noise and stir." "The pleasure of solitude is a thing incomprehensible."[10] Above all, we aim to stay motivated.

It should then come as a comfort that in surveying the wisdom of the Christian tradition, we find that a trinity of spiritual dispositions, silence, stillness, and waiting, animates true piety. These dispositions are meant to restore our frenzied selves to wholeness, vitality, and mindfulness of mystery. For those who wish to deny our troubled situation, they may seem odd, or counter-productive, maybe even a waste of time. But as we observe in scripture and tradition these are also qualities of the triune God.

To be sure, we must be careful in talking about this trinity of spiritual dispositions. At green retreats and plush resorts, affluent men and women move languorously through quiet days, luxuriating in the balm of affluence. In my southern childhood, most of us in the white churches were quite content to remain still and silent in response to the urgencies of racism and civil rights. Faced with the moral imperatives of our time—social justice for the disenfranchised, the reform of a complacent and acquiescent church—we opted for the country clubs, for summer cotillions, and for the secure spaces of segregated schools, churches and neighborhoods. We took refuge in serene detachment. Stillness can be a polite form of indifference or self-indulgence.

THE PSALMIST INVITES US into a stillness that focuses energy, clarifies vision, and teaches us to listen anew to God, to others, and ourselves. "Be still and know that I am God." Jesus calms the stormy sea with the words, "Peace, be still!"

Bonhoeffer wrote in *Life Together*:

> Silence is the simple stillness of the individual under the Word of God. We are silent at the beginning of the day because God should have the first word, and we are silent before going to sleep because the last word also belongs to God. We keep silence solely for the sake of the Word, and therefore not in order to show disregard for the Word but rather to honor and receive it. . . . The silence of the Christian is listening silence, humble stillness. . . . It is silence in conjunction with the Word.[11]

Be still *and know*: the stillness of the man and woman before the word nurtures a respectful attention to the world, to pain and suffering, beauty and splendor, an attunement to a deeper mundane.[12] In stillness, we no longer come to God as *deus ex machina*, that fine idea that rescues us from uncertainty and dread; we learn instead to be open to the one who loves, frees, and heals, and thus responsive to the mystery of the world. In stillness before the word, we are given time to see God, not necessarily in mystical apprehension, but through the deep transformation of our perceptions of life. *Being still and knowing* enables us to see with heightened awareness the concrete places in the world that cry out for wholeness and re-demptive action, "to see everything in a new light," as the Catholic philosopher Joseph Pieper wrote, "to see the deeper visage of the real so that the attention directed to the things encountered in everyday experience comes up against what is not so obvious in these things."[13] This kind of seeing gives rise to wonder and wor-ship, flooding the soul with tenderness and compassion.

We must take care when we talk about silence, for there are many dangerous silences. There is silence of the bystander and of the ones whose voices have been silenced. There is silent re-treat from responsible action.

These are not the silences of the word. In the Old Testament, God's election of Moses to usher in Israel's deliverance from captivity began with a lesson in how to talk about God. "And God said unto Moses, I AM THAT I AM: and he said, Thus shalt thou say unto the children of Israel, I AM hath sent me unto you" (Exod. 3:14 KJV). Respectful speaking of God makes space for the holy; it keeps the mystery in a listening humility. "Who gives speech to mortals?" the Lord asks Moses. "Who gives wisdom and knowledge?"[14]

God tells the prophet Isaiah that the nation's festivals and solemn assemblies, its rallies and noisy hosts, its incense and of-ferings, "have become a burden to me." "I am weary of hearing them" (Isa. 1:14). God is tired even of their prayers.[15]

Beholding the righteousness of God, the prophet Zechariah says: "Be silent, O all flesh, before the LORD for he is raised up out of his holy habitation" (Zech. 2:13).

In *Life Together*, Bonhoeffer spoke of a stillness "before the Word" and a stillness that "comes from the Word." He affirmed the wisdom of the psalmist, the importance of a listening silence, the "wonderful power of clarification, purification, and concentration upon the essential thing."[16]

There is also a silence that disrupts the smooth exchanges of power and aggression. Silence can stop the world in its tracks: the silent response to the cruel joke, the intolerable silence of dissent. Silence may betoken an invitation to question, or take the form of a question itself. It is often not the spoken word that brands a person an outsider or agitator, but a manner of silence that exposes the mob opinion as a lie. Truthful speech emerges out of silence more often than out of noise. In her book, *Keeping God's Silence: Towards a Theological Ethics of Communication*, the British Quaker theologian Nancy Muers describes holy silence as a "listening unto speech." This means learning to listen to the other person, allowing a silent or silenced other to speak, a listening silence.[17]

We may also speak of the silence of gratitude and wonder. In the encounter of a great work of art, quietness and attunement precede the activity of interpretation and imitation. Wonder, languor, bewilderment, inspiration—we stand in a receptive silence. In the silence, we experience the work as a truth that transcends our own place, and we are called out of ourselves. In response to the gift of salvation—and what gift is more precious than the gift of freeing love—it is better if I am left choosing my words carefully, sometimes with difficulty. "Let all mortal flesh keep silence," reads the *Book of Common Prayer*. And sometimes we are left speechless, and that is as it should be. It should probably be that way more often.

"If we are to learn what God promises, and what God fulfills," Bonhoeffer wrote in prison to his dear friend Eberhard Bethge, "we must persevere in quiet meditation on the life, sayings, deeds, sufferings, and the death of Jesus."[18] There is the silence of deliberate, prayerful attention to the way of Christ.

Holy silence is thus not compensation for the deficiency of the word. For the word is not deficient; it is abundance and joy. The word creates its own surplus and is never wanting; the word fills and overfills, awakens and astonishes. It invites us to a refreshing silence. (One would also say it "awes," except that awe, so apt a description of God's amazing grace, has been stripped of dignity by the world's most powerful military—the shock and awe of high-tech invasion and mass death.)

"Wait for the Lord; be strong, and let your heart take courage; wait for the Lord!" Here, in Psalm 27:14, we are admonished to be strong and take heart; strength and courage are qualities of living faith. We are not told to be weak and timid. Strength and courage are found in waiting on the Lord; for stillness and silence are original qualities of the holiness of the Lord. The sense in the passage is that of learning to participate in God's beauty and holiness and to accept God's love as a gift. Waiting on the Lord means "dwelling in the house," "gazing upon the beauty of the Lord," "seeking God in his temple," "keeping safe in his dwelling," and "hiding in the shelter of his tabernacle" (Ps. 27).

WAITING ON THE LORD DOES NOT FOLLOW a technique or formula. Waiting is the light of gratitude, the simple, grateful acceptance of grace where true piety begins. "God is not looking for heroic figures—wonderful people—who captivate others with their charisma," wrote Christoph Blumhardt, the nineteenth-century pastor and peacemaker.[19] The basic question is: "Are you living in the reality of Jesus Christ?" This question shifts the focus of discipleship from mighty actions in pursuit of spiritual perfection to simple trust in Christ and just actions. "Can you take [the reality of Jesus Christ] into your life?" Blumhardt asks, "Can you let it guide your whole life, even in the midst of the deepest suffering?" Gratitude stills our hearts, relieves us of our messianic ambitions; gratitude means freedom. Waiting is trusting.

At the same time, waiting on the word and being still before the word teaches us humility about the way we speak to God. God is the author of our faith, and the source of all truth and meaning. Christians do not need to offer an answer to every question, and God does not expect us to. It is so much easier to blurt out a ripe opinion than to wait for God and listen to others. We may try to orchestrate the work of the kingdom and impose our cleverness on the Spirit, but God invites us to wait. Accept his love and rest inside it.

As a father of three children, I am quick to respond to the needs of my children with the offer of more activity and more diversions. But listening closely, I realize that what they really want—not always but often—is to be present with me.

We might also think of waiting on the Lord in stillness and silence as an echo of the church's anticipation of the return of Jesus Christ. We live in the "time of the between," in the second part of a three-part drama. In scripture and in tradition we are taught the way this drama will end, with the breaking-in of a new heaven and a new earth, with the glory of the "new Jerusalem, coming down out of heaven" (Rev. 21:2). We know the way the drama will end because we have been shown the first act, the demolition of the "nothing" on the cross, the sealing of the promise of salvation, the defeat of Satan. Yet we live in the time between the abandonment of Good Friday and the glory of Easter Sunday morning, in the Saturday of the between.[20] "We live," Barth says, "amidst transition—a transition from death to life, from the unrighteousness of men to the righteousness of God, from the old to the new creation."[21] In this between time, which the church dares to call Holy Saturday, our witness as Christians will be most clear and compelling when it grows out of the simple desire to abide with Christ, and when our action emerges out of an expectant waiting.

I HOPE IT IS QUITE CLEAR now that our season of silence is not a time of removing the words of faith from our lips: sin, grace, cross, forgiveness, reconciliation, resurrection. That sad remedy has been tried before by Christians seeking entry into secular culture, the effort to gain respect by giving up on miracle and metaphysics, but that remedy does nothing to nourish the mission of the church. The call to silence is rather a summons to mindfulness and depth, to forsake the corrosive habits of hurried and half-considered talk. It is a call to daily, personal encounter with the crucified and resurrected Christ to live in the fullness of the Holy Spirit, to discern the moment's resplendence against the horizon of grace. Such concentration will not be easy but it is necessary, for it is the depth and the silence of God out of which our words must arise ever anew. The word will be reborn not by repetition but "by an inspiration that reopens it."[22] Certainly none of us can live our whole lives inside this concentration, but we must remain there awhile in hopes that afterwards much will be changed in our lives—and we must return there when our words grow tired.

How will we know what to say and do? Will all this attention to the mindfulness of speech lead to a paralysis of thought? Am I guilty of excessive scrupulousness, promoting an unhealthy self-awareness that will only produce anxious speech?

In response to our fears and uncertainties, Jesus invites us to listen in order that we may learn how to speak. "What I tell you in the dark," Jesus says, "speak in the daylight; what is whispered in your ear, proclaim from the housetops" (Matt. 10:27 NIV). Jesus whispers the secret. The gospel is a precious gift. Behold its beauty in a listening silence. Taste and see its loveliness. Let it permeate your hearts and minds. At the same time, the gospel must be spoken in the daylight, shouted from the rooftops, and proclaimed to the powers in high places. Though we are surrounded by conflicts, anxieties, and doubts, though we face persecution, the peace that passes all understanding dwells in our midst. We must learn to be silent, but we must not take refuge in silence. There is a time to cover and conceal, and there is a time of uncovering and illumination. We cannot be silent forever. But we must take care that our shouting from the housetops never overwhelms the whispering of Jesus.

Stillness before the word thus means being formed as hearers, as those who strain to hear the present moment against the faint chorus of the angels' singing.[23] Stillness means learning to be quiet in a noisy nation, to reexamine our lives, as Bonhoeffer said, in a time of "purification, clarification and concentration upon the essential thing." Stillness means learning to speak in such way that the healing word of God is able to be heard again and experienced in the world. The psychiatrist Paul Tournier notes the priority of silence in psychoanalysis: Waiting for a word, one often receives silence, and in the silence a language is born and in that new language come understanding and healing.[24] In the end, silence means learning to wait on God's word and to receive from God's word a blessing.[25] The heart of waiting lies deep in the silence of prayer. Lord, teach us to pray.

Holy silence is not then the withdrawal of religion from the public square, the sort recommended by the philosopher Richard Rorty, who regards all religious claims as "conversation stoppers" and inherently irrational.[26] Holy silence is shaped rather by a passion for faith's integrity, and it seeks to protect and preserve the mysteries of faith in acts of compassion, in prayer, fellowship, liturgy, devotional life, and worship. We might think of holy silence as a season of concentrated attention to faith's essential affirmations during which we bear witness to the authenticity of faith in the practices we keep: showing hospitality to strangers and outcasts; affirming the unity of the created order; reclaiming the ideals of beauty, love, honesty, and truth; embracing the preferential option for non-violence; learning to live in the world in a way that is participatory rather than manipulative; remembering the simple tasks of visiting the widows and the orphans in their distress; being slow to speak and slow to anger; being quick to listen.[27]

The good news is that God invites us—broken, fragile, and creative people, longing for wholeness—to join him on a journey of new beginnings. God invites us to join him in friendship in the community of his love. Our acceptance is not conditioned by our moral perfection or heroic feats, or by the willingness to offer up our self-identities on a silver platter. God asks for gratitude, as God seeks us out as participants in a new community, the community established in grace. The sincerity of our gratitude is a matter of our willingness to accept the invitation and of learning to be content in the mystery of small and ordinary things.

Can we in the churches find our way back from propaganda and equivocation to singleness of mind? What we will need are men

and women who are passionately and irrepressibly human, lacking
deviousness and deception, willing to admit mistakes and to rethink options from the perspective of new life in Christ. "What we
shall need," Bonhoeffer said, "is not geniuses, or cynics, or misanthropes, or clever tacticians, but plain, honest, straightforward
people."[28] In a time such as ours, when the gospel of Jesus Christ
has been so often reduced to partisan talking points and when too
much Christian talk in the public square has served to humiliate
the word rather than to bring glory to God, learning to be still and
wait, learning to abide with Jesus in the Garden of Gethsemane,
may be our only hope for the discernment we will need in the uncertain years ahead.

Chapter Eight
PASSING THE INTERNATIONAL TEST
The Call of Global Christianity

IN THE 2004 ELECTION DEBATES, the Democratic nominee, John Kerry, criticized President George W. Bush's decision to launch preemptive war against Iraq on the grounds that it failed to pass the "global test." Kerry's point was that before authorizing a preemptive strike, an American president should be obligated to make the moral case to the international community. The president who commits the nation's military to war should carefully explain "to the world that [he] did it for legitimate reasons."

The issue of "the global test" quickly became a subject of wide-ranging ridicule among Christian and non-Christian conservatives. Senator Kerry was accused of endorsing the treasonous notion that American foreign policy should be subject to the approval of intemperate nations such as France. Few conservatives in those days were having kind thoughts about the people who brought us the *philosophes*, Jean-Paul Sartre, and freedom fries. Kerry's sin was that of asking America to respect the views of other democracies when making foreign policy decisions that affected global stability. Senator Kerry had the audacity to suggest that the United States should act in consideration of the world community, that our nation dare not behave as a fully autonomous power accountable to no one.

I will let others address the future of the foreign policy that led us to the crisis in Iraq. What weighs heavily on my mind are the serious theological costs of the ecclesial indifference to the "global test." No doubt, it is in the nature of partisan self-promotion to exploit the public meanings and connotations of an opponent's remarks for strategic benefit. But Christians are to be people who are defined first and foremost by citizenship in the kingdom of God. We are not only obligated to pass a global test, but we are defined by one—and indeed by a supra-global test!

The earliest writings of the Christian tradition gave voice to the transnational identity of the faith community. In one of his most widely quoted meditations on the new identity of the Christian, Saint Paul writes that "as many of you who were baptized into Christ have put on Christ," there is now "neither Jew nor Greek, there is neither male nor female, for you are all one in Christ Jesus" (Gal. 3:27–28 WEB). Paul's explorations of life "in Christ" amplify the theme of the "new creation" and the new being's capacity to cross boundaries and to reshape loyalties. Baptism is the sacrament that brings the person into the body of Christ, which is, among other things, an alternative social world. "For by one Spirit are we all baptized into one body, whether we be Jews or Gentiles, whether we be bond or free; and have been all made to drink into one Spirit" (1 Cor. 12:13).

Other early Christian writers echoed Paul's Christ-centered cosmopolitanism. "We acknowledge one all-embracing commonwealth—the world," the patristic theologian Tertullian wrote in

The Apology.[1] The third-century document *The Life and Passion of Cyprian, Bishop and Martyr*, by Pontius the Deacon, states similarly: "To the Christian, the whole of this world is one home." Saint Augustine says in *The City of God* that "the heavenly city" in its sojourn on earth calls citizens out of all nations and "gathers together a society of pilgrims of all languages."[2]

The affirmation of the transnational character of the body of Christ was not a mere theological fancy; it was grounded in the demographical realities of the new Christian religion. Of the five ancient patriarchates of the church, only one was in the West, and that was Rome.[3] Three were on the Asian continent, in Constantinople, Antioch, and Jerusalem, and one was in Africa, in Alexandria. Many of the great early leaders of the Christian faith, who helped define the central convictions of the faith, Tertullian and Augustine, Cyprian and Athanasius, among many other formative influences in the development of Christianity, lived on the African continent. Therefore, Christianity was never only a European or Western religion.[4] Even today, the Christian community in Ethiopia, after decades of conflicts with Muslims and Marxists, includes more than twenty million members, five times the size of the Episcopal Church in the United States. A Christian community of nearly a million lived in Iraq under Saddam Hussein's repressive regime. However, few of us in the evangelical churches asked the Christians in Iraqi churches what they thought of our plan for the Middle East.[5]

In his essential book *The Next Christendom: The Coming of Global Christianity*, historian Philip Jenkins looks closely at the important shifts in world Christian populations that have taken place over the past century and at their impact for Christians in the West. He describes a new religious landscape in terms that may surprise many. For example, the typical contemporary Christian is not a suburban white conservative or an urban religious progressive. If we want to visualize this contemporary Christian, Jenkins says, we should think instead of a woman living in a village in Nigeria or in a Brazilian slum. In recent decades, the center of gravity in the Christian world has shifted dramatically southward to Asia, Latin America, and Africa. The largest Christian communities in the world today are found in Africa and Latin America, and the trend points toward a global majority of non-white, non-Western Christians within a few decades.[6] According to Jenkins, by the year 2050, only one-fifth of the world's three billion Christians will be non-Hispanic whites. Yet, amidst all the dramatic change in the landscape of world Christianity, the Western churches have not fully reckoned with the important ways these changes inspire us to reconsider their identity and mission.[7]

The significance of Jenkins's analysis for Christianity in North America is that, at the very least, the recognition of an emergent world Christianity should chasten our presumption to speak of the Christian faith on the basis of our own preferences. This is not to suggest that new Christian communities in the southern hemisphere are left-leaning or progressive in their politics. Jenkins claims that contrary to the conventional academic wisdom—namely, that these Third World Christians would introduce the West to a new revolutionary vanguard raised on liberation theology and Marxist interpretations of the Bible—the most-rapidly growing churches are traditional Roman Catholic and evangelical Protestant or Pentecostal. "Southern Christians retain a very strong supernatural orientation," he says, "and are by and large far more interested in personal salvation than radical politics."

The new world Christians defy familiar political description. They support social justice and economic redistribution, but they also work out their faith with an exuberant sense of the supernatural and the miraculous. More often than not they live in poverty, while deriving their social analysis from the biblical narratives of exile and deliverance, which they read in terms of both spiritual allegory and real historical hope. Pentecostalism, which remains the fastest growing of all new Christian communities, further confronts us with a dazzling mix of otherworldliness, multiracialism, faith-healing, biblical literalism, and social uplift. Jenkins is correct in his claim that liberal Western observers are not inclined to find the ideological tone of the new churches to their liking. Even so, despite the global church's theological conservativism, the vast majority of the new congregations opposed the American invasion of Iraq—although as we will see in more detail later in this chapter, few in our country were ever told this, thanks to both the mainline and evangelical media.

I am not suggesting that we should romanticize the new world Christian communities, or *tout court* privilege the foreign over the familiar. There is no reason to think that the insights of a theologically untrained African are more truthful expressions of the Christian faith than those of a philosophical theologian in the North American academy. There is nothing in the nature of cultural difference per se that corrects the errors of identity. I once had a suitemate at Harvard Divinity School from West Africa who thought that our neighbor's epileptic seizure was a sign of demonic possession. The African student was a dear man, and I learned much from him. Yet certainly such a dangerously unenlightened notion of neurological diseases highlights the need to bring balance to our estimation of the "other." Global Christianity does not save Western Christians from the intellectual challenges of the Enlightenment and the discoveries of science.

However, the emergent world communities undoubtedly offer perspectives and insights which may help discipline the messianic impulse of the American church. As Philip Jenkins says, "Considering Christianity as a global reality can make us see the whole religion in a radically new perspective, which is startling and, often, uncomfortable." In particular, the rise of global Christianity offers American Christians much-needed training in spiritual humility. Most Christians in the world are not white and suburban, black and urban, or black and suburban. Most Christians are not Republican or Democrat, readers of *Christianity Today* or *Sojourners*. Most Christians do not lay claim to expanding territories nor enjoy the sounds of a praise band. Rather, most Christians in the world are poor, often desperately so, and many are persecuted.

ANOTHER ASTUTE OBSERVER of global Christianity is the Gambia native and Yale professor Lamin Sanneh, who has described "post-Western Christianity" and the "worldwide Christian resurgences" as developments that challenge the myopic worldview of North American Christians, especially the presumption that our political and cultural conceptions are normative for the global church. However, Sanneh pays more attention than Jenkins to the theological lessons for North American Christians.

In his book *Whose Religion Is Christianity? The Gospel beyond the West*, Sanneh argues that in the current global revival,

Christians in the United States are presented with a rare opportunity to recall the circumstances and conditions that gave birth to the church as "a divine office" rather than as "a political institution."[8] Sanneh detects in the rise of world Christianity little evidence of "global pretensions" aligned along the dominant political agendas. "World Christianity" is reminiscent of the early church, which existed not only on the margins of political power but in a state of constant assault by the worldly powers. The early church represented a new social order, an alternative to the dominant society determined by privilege and hierarchy. There was "no entrance fee for membership" into these communities, because it was understood that the kingdom of God was "especially for the least among us." Sanneh thinks that the new global churches point us back to the counter-cultural origins of the Christian faith when the church existed precisely to welcome men and women "who have eaten of the bread of adversity and tasted the waters of affliction" into the kingdom of God.

American civil religion, on the other hand, in its wholesome middle-class forms, interweaves the saving story of the gospel with the story of American greatness and is thus really part of the larger problem of modern liberal Christianity (as I discussed earlier). Sanneh analyzes the problem as a reduction of the mystery of God "to a cultural filibuster." The Christian feels free to remold the good news of Jesus Christ according to cultural preferences and needs. The recognition that these preferences and needs (which no doubt comfort and inspire us with a sense of providential specialness) are but human constructions influenced by prejudice may come as a shock, but it should not leave us in despair. The recognition opens us up to a richer and more vital connection to the body of Christ: The church becomes an authentic expression of the whole body of Christ only when people of differing nations and traditions plumb together the length and breadth and height and depth of the love of God (see Eph. 3:14–19).[9]

M Y FRIEND MARK GORNIK is a Presbyterian minister and dean of the recently founded City Seminary in Harlem. Aside from his duties in academic administration and pastoral ministry, Reverend Gornik has invested considerable time over the past five years studying the rise of immigrant churches in the five boroughs of New York. He is writing a doctoral dissertation on top of everything else. In the spring of 2004, the *New York Times* featured his research on world Christianity and globalization in a front-page Sunday feature story entitled, "Where the Gospel Resounds in African Tongues."[10] He has undertaken this ambitious project with the sensitivity of a loving pastor and the tenacity of a skilled ethnographer, discovering many of the new immigrant congregations on block-by-block walks in the boroughs, since many of the congregations have no listed phone number. In his effort to understand the story of the revival on the margins, Gornik has counted more than two hundred new African churches in the city. The lessons of his research are essential for evangelical and mainline congregations in United States.

The African immigrant churches in New York, like most churches affected by the cross-cultural diffusion of the gospel, follow the story line found in the Acts of the Apostles, the action-packed New Testament narrative of the first Christian communities. The plot of Acts tells of the church growing quickly multicultural in the first generation, attracting diverse people to Jesus who worship together in ever more culturally inclusive forms. Importantly, neither in the early Christian churches nor in New York today is religious transformation a result of top-down decisions by elites. Transformation results "from grassroots movements and the initiative of people from around the world."[11] This "globalization of the spirit" Gornik sees exemplified both in the flourishing immigrant congregations in New York (and throughout the United States) and in global Christianity. It offers an urgently needed Sunday-school lesson for American Christians. The lesson is this:

"We are not at the center of the Christian world," Gornik says. "The global Christian movement is not the American story, as difficult as that might be for us to hear. We are not in control of the church."[12]

Reverend Gornik also thinks that the stories of new immigrant communities in the urban centers of the West can help reeducate American Christians on the basic purpose of the church in the world; namely that "the diaspora is the mission." Christians too often assume that their mission is to build and fortify permanent institutional structures, but these immigrant churches remind Christians of their calling to live in the world as pilgrim people. Learning to live as though "diaspora" itself were the mission challenges the way we think about the Christian life. Christians are scattered and dispersed.

I would also note that white evangelicals can learn these lessons by looking more closely at the story of African American Christianity, not only as history but as spiritual instruction on being a peculiar people. In his essential essay "American Salvation: The Place of Christianity in Public Life," published in the *Boston Review* in the spring of 2005, the Princeton historian and religious scholar Albert J. Raboteau argued that African American Christianity has "continuously confronted the nation with troubling questions about American exceptionalism." The story of the African American journey centers on "suffering-slave Christianity" and makes "a prophetic condemnation of America's obsession with power, status, and possessions."[13] Raboteau writes, "African-American Christians perceived in American exceptionalism a dangerous tendency to turn the nation into an idol and Christianity into a clan religion." But this is a distorted notion of biblical Christianity. In biblical Christianity, divine election does not bring "preeminence, elevation and glory, but—as black Christians know all too well—humiliation, suffering, and rejection." "Chosenness, as reflected in the life of Jesus," Raboteau continues, "led to a cross. The lives of the disciples have been signed with that cross. To be chosen, in this perspective, means joining company not with the powerful and the rich but with those who suffer: the outcast, the poor, and the despised."[14]

Gornik thinks that the failure of privileged American Christians to join company with those who suffer and endure persecution has severely damaged the church's credibility.

"The problem with white evangelicals in U.S. is that they do not get outside of their own culture," Gornik says. "They lack inquisitiveness. And that lack of inquisitiveness is killing the church, and it's killing the country."

"We are incomplete as Christians if we are culturally isolated," he adds. "We are not the people we should be."[15]

Gornik calls the rise of immigrant churches in New York "an Ephesians moment." To illustrate the point, he offers the "subway test" as evidence. On his daily subway rides, Gornik likes to look around the car to see who is reading the Bible. New York City is often regarded as the great secular metropolis, but Gornik finds signs of renewal in the ordinary and sometimes forgotten places of the city. On subway cars in Harlem he sees men and women, teenagers and children, reading Scripture or devotional books. Sometimes they are standing with one hand on the guardrail with the other clutching a pocket-size New Testament. Usually these people are African, Hispanic, or Christians from other new immigrant communities in the city.

Gornik thinks that believers in North America urgently need to grasp the significance of the monumental changes through which they are living: the center of gravity in global Christianity is fast shifting from the north to the south. These new Christians in the southern hemisphere, with their intense spiritual energies for holiness and mission, are God's reminder that the kingdom of God is a world movement. Growing in the faith and living with a greater mindfulness of the kingdom means reckoning ever more fully with the new shape of the church.

MY PARENTS HAVE SPENT much of the past fifteen years working in English-speaking congregations in Europe. They have lived in Copenhagen, Vienna, Stuttgart, Zurich, Frankfurt, and most recently Berlin. Like Mark Gornik, my parents have come to see the importance of the global test. Their ministry in these western cities has given them a perspective on American Christianity that, I think, offers the evangelical churches important insights.

My father is a Southern Baptist preacher who served congregations in Alabama, Mississippi, and Georgia over a forty-year career before beginning ministry abroad. Though he considers himself a political conservative, my father understands that his commitment to the gospel chastens many of his own cultural and political preferences. He opposes abortion but supports gun control and universal health care. He voted for George W. Bush in 2000 and 2004, but admires Jimmy Carter and Bill Clinton (whom he voted for in 1992), both of whom are Baptists from the Deep South.[16] My father has always brought a passion for foreign missions to the churches he has served in small towns and large cities. Working in European congregations for the past decade has made him more aware of the vital spiritual importance of an international frame of reference.

Many of my father's letters to me over the past years read like testimonies of the global body of Christ. He considers his time in Europe as the most rewarding period of his life in ministry and is grateful for the time spent with the diverse and vital memberships of his English-speaking international congregations. In March 2002, he wrote of a Sunday morning in Frankfurt and of the joy he found in worshiping with Christians from around the world. The congregation that day included "the new director for the American Embassy, a woman from Burma, an Austrian psychologist, an opera singer from Mexico, two newcomers from Iran, another from the Philippines, another from Somalia, two more from Austria, and three from African countries. At least 20 different nations were represented. The worship center was filled, and the spirit of praise and wonder was precious."[17]

By the spring of 2003, however, my father's letters and phone calls from Europe began to note the dramatically altering perceptions of American evangelical Christianity among international members of the congregations where he was ministering. In one letter he told me of a German woman in Berlin who approached him after a service. She thanked him for his presentation of the gospel and his skillful way of making the Bible come alive and feel personal. Then she asked, "But if I accept Jesus Christ as my Lord and Savior, do I also have to support George W. Bush"? The woman was not being sarcastic.

Like most expats, my parents have experienced their share of anti-American sentiment in Europe and elsewhere in their travels abroad. But the intensity of criticism, concern, and anger encountered in recent years by parishioners and neighbors has given them pause to reconsider the new and deeply disturbing challenges facing Christian ministers and missionaries abroad. Like the woman in Berlin, most internationals have come to regard evangelical Christianity as the theological shell of the Republican Party. My father was sobered by her question.

He remembers with shame and sadness the situation of the southern churches in the United States in the 1960s, when the work of Baptist missions in the global south but especially in Africa were greatly hampered by the racism of their home churches in the States. As a Southern Baptist missionary wrote to his state denominational newspaper, "What you do and say in America today is speaking so loud our people around the world are finding it more difficult to hear what we say. Our people listen to the radio. They read the newspaper. And some even have television. They know what is happening today. It is impossible to explain why a black person can't worship in a Baptist church in America when you send us out here to tell them that Jesus loves them."[18] In their work in Europe, my parents have been saddened to discover how seriously the missionary enterprise has been undermined by the "myopic mindset" of American Christendom.

"We need to circle the word 'global' and think it through," my father said. "Too many of us still think that Christianity is American, and that America is the best and most pure nation in the world. That sounds a lot like the way we used to think about the South."

My father realizes that the partisan captivity of the gospel has become the new stumbling block to the Christian commission of making disciples of all nations, baptizing them in the name of the Father, Son, and Holy Spirit, and teaching them to obey the commands of Jesus.

"Why have we not taken seriously the teachings of Jesus when he said that His disciples should be peacemakers? I'm pretty sure He meant what He said. The prophets had a vision of a world where swords would be beaten into plows. I hope and pray that our churches will recapture that vision: a kingdom where violence is unthinkable, and a Kingdom where all people humble themselves before God."

In January 2006, I wrote an editorial in the *New York Times* called "Wayward Christian Soldiers," which was critical of American evangelical support for war in Iraq. The editorial struck a nerve; not only was it the most widely emailed article of the month, but in response, I received more than five hundred letters, many written by American Christians overseas eager to express their gratitude for a dissenting voice within the evangelical community. Most of these also shared their dismay at the behavior of conservative Christians in the United States. A missionary living in Singapore noted that every time our president makes a foreign policy decision, the ministers serving communities in that country "hold their breath." Another wrote of his visit to a conservative think tank in Washington in the fall of 2005. He was asked by a State Department official what our government could do to reduce persecution of Christians around the world. The missionary replied, "Go slowly and gather intelligence from Christians living far away from the corridors of power." Take the time to "listen to indigenous believers" around the world, to their perspectives on American power and its effect on the unsaved. "But I'm not sure if the audience understood what I meant," he said. The missionary recalled being met with blank stares. Another Christian from the U.S. who had lived on three different continents over three decades observed that while believers in other places "might not be as schooled" as some of our pastors, they nonetheless live out their faith "in a wide sense." "It may be that sometimes North American Christians are North American first, and only Christian later."

Evangelicals in the U.S. have increasingly isolated themselves from shared faith with the global church, practicing an ecumenical isolationism that mirrors the political trend. But as we have seen, a Christian cannot live as an isolationist, indifferent to an international perspective, because every Christian community is, theologically, an ecumenical fellowship. Every Christian community is at one with all other Christian communities in all other places, nations and regions, whether or not the Christians in a local community recognize this theological fact or like it.[19] Our individual preferences must be tempered by our consideration of the global communion of believers. "Independence has always been balanced by mutual accountability," wrote the evangelical theologian and Anglican bishop N. T. Wright in October 2003.[20] The Georgia Baptist preacher Clarence Jordan liked to say that the steeple is defined by the kingdom, that every local congregation represents a point of entry into the global fellowship of the church, despite the intentions of particular memberships to take refuge in sameness. When one steps into the local church, even into the most culturally homogeneous congregation, one enters into a transnational association of astonishing diversity. The purpose of preaching today must be then to remind Christians of this theological fact. Is it not then time for Christians in the

United States to affirm the universal fellowship of the Church and to rethink their identities on the basis of the Body of Christ?

This affirmation is as old as the first book of the Bible. In the creation story in the book of Genesis, we learn that God created man and woman in his own image: "in the image of God he created them—male and female." A divine image, or spark—the *imago dei*—as the Latin Fathers of the church called it, ensures the dignity of human life and makes unacceptable the denial of any person's created dignity. John Calvin, despite his healthy appreciation of the fall's pervasive affects, regarded God's creation of man and woman as the "noblest and most reasonable example of his justice, wisdom and goodness."[21]

In the Christian doctrine of the incarnation, we further learn that all reality—and all creation in its detail and diversity—is taken up into Jesus Christ and linked together in him, so that now, as Bonhoeffer said in *Ethics,* human history becomes the story of "divergence" and "convergence" in relation to its new center.[22] This means that the great event of the cross and the resurrection enables us to affirm the interconnectedness of humanity and creation as the result of a specific redemptive act. Still, there are also times when the church must lay aside concern for its specificity and distinctiveness and offer clear and unequivocal testimony to the interdependence of all humanity created in God's image, indeed, when such universal affirmations must be regarded as part of a life of costly discipleship. This does not mean that Christians abandon their devotion to Jesus; it means rather that following Jesus leads us to an invigorated humanism, a humanism realized for the sake of the gospel. There are times when the Christian church should sing *with* the nations, "one love, one blood . . . one life with each other . . . sisters, brothers," as in the words of U2's stirring global anthem. Now is most assuredly one of those times.

If the kingdom of God is the place where the world is shown its real history—the coming of the peace that passes all understanding—then such affirmations should not be difficult. They should feel like a refreshing breeze, full of hope, joy, energy, and light (like a U2 concert, as my students would say). The burden is simply too great for one nation or one church (one part of the one body) to cheerily go it alone, scoffing at the global test. "For in fact the body is not one member but many," Saint Paul wrote in his first letter to the new church in Corinth, "and if one member suffers, all the members suffer with it; or if one member is honored, all the members rejoice with it. Now you are the body of Christ, and members individually" (12:14, 26–27 NKJV). Because we belong to the body of Christ, we belong also to the world.

LET US ASK AGAIN: At what cost to our witness in the world and the integrity of our message did evangelicals gain their political access and power? Have we become distinguished more by self-righteousness than passion for the righteousness of God? Have we presumed the authority to tweak the gospel to fit our needs, shown contempt for the Lordship of Jesus Christ over the church and all creation, contempt even for the saints and the martyrs? To be sure, we can give conclusive answers to every perplexing issue of our time—just ask us, we'll tell you. We have met the age of relativism with an empire of certainties. But we are not better Christians for it; we have failed to live as ambassadors of reconciliation. We have not loved God with our whole heart, we have not loved our neighbors as ourselves, but we are not truly sorry and have not humbly repented. The church cannot preach salvation to the nations while showing contempt for the nations.

Rush Limbaugh may have pleased his "Dittoheads" in mocking the dissenting pastors, archbishops, bishops, and church leaders from other countries who stuck their noses into our foreign policy. But the men and women in the U.S. who call themselves Christian and have been baptized into the body of Christ are judged according to a different standard than that of blasphemous malcontents. Why did American evangelicals not pause for a moment in the rush to war to consider the near-unanimous disapproval of the preemptive attack by the global Christian community? While such influential conservatives as Charles Colson, Bill Bright, James Kennedy, and Richard Land were signing a letter of support for the president's decision to invade Iraq, Christian leaders around the world—evangelical, orthodox, and liberal—were expressing their dismay over the administration's case.[23] The global Christian opposition seems to me the most neglected story related to the religious debate about Iraq: Despite the 87 percent approval of white evangelicals in April of 2003 for the president's decision to go to war, almost every Christian leader in the world (and almost every non-evangelical leader in the United States) voiced opposition to the war.

The statements, declarations, and petitions that were drafted by the international Christian community read like a litany for the global church and an indictment of the myopic mindset of American evangelicalism. Listen to the voices of our brothers and sisters in the ecumenical church:

> It is with profound sadness that we follow the news of the
> start of yet another war that plagues the region of the world

in which our church lives and ministers. . . . We affirm the Christian principle of peace and reconciliation that was sacrificially personified by our Lord and Savior Jesus Christ.

—Union of Armenian Evangelical Churches in the
Near East, March 22, 2003

We, the officers of the Christian Conference of Asia, an ecumenical organization of more than 100 churches in Asia, consisting of more than 50 million individual Christians, join the world community in expressing disapproval and condemnation of the war against Iraq.

—Christian Conference of Asia, March 20, 2003

The war will cause intense, irreparable damage to life and the planet. It will also affect the situation of the already badly hit population of Iraq and will widen the abyss between people from different cultures and creeds.

—The Ecumenical Service Coordinator, Brazil,
March 19, 2003

We, the International Movement of Catholic Students and the International Young Catholic Students in communion with Pope John Paul II and countless other religious leaders, wish to express our stance against the current illegal and immoral war on Iraq.

—International Movement of Catholic Students
(PaxRomana), April 11, 2003

The events of recent days show that doubts still persist about the moral legitimacy as well as the unpredictable humanitarian consequences of a war with Iraq.

—Church of England, February 20, 2003

As people of faith, our love of neighbor compels us to oppose war and to seek peaceful resolution of conflicts . . .
Pre-emptive military strike and war as a means to change
the regime of a sovereign state are immoral and in violation
of the UN Charter.

> —Conference of European Churches,
> February 2, 3003

We deplore the fact that the most powerful nations of this
world again regard war as an acceptable instrument of foreign policy. This creates an international culture of fear,
threat and insecurity. We cannot accept the stated objec-
tives of a war against Iraq, as laid out by these governments,
in particular the U.S. pre-emptive military strike and war
as means to change the regime of a sovereign state.

> —Evangelical Church of Germany, February 5, 2003

The billions of dollars that are being channeled to destroy
human lives and property in the war could have been used
to help alleviate suffering, which could have resulted in
promoting a more peaceful world than we are experiencing
at the moment.

> —Christian Council of Ghana, March 26, 2003

From the historic city founded by Alexander the Great and
where Christianity was preached by St. Mark the Apostle
and Evangelist; from the land of the Nile river and a country which is a model and example of harmony between
Christians and Muslims, I wish to make an earnest call to
Your Excellency [President George W. Bush] to avoid any
attacks on Iraq.

> —Greek Orthodox Church of Alexandria and
> All Africa, January 2, 2003

This is a time of fear and sorrow for many . . . The voices of Churches, and millions of people of good will, opposing the immoral and illegal use of force were unheard . . . The war causes, in our region and well beyond, great pain and danger. It must stop. As people of faith, this is our cry today.

> —Greek Orthodox Patriarchate of Antioch and All the East, March 25, 2003

The ongoing War creates a culture of fear, threat and insecurity.

> —The National Council of Churches in India, April 1, 2003

The war has begun, and we will begin counting the dead, the victims, and the injured. . . . We live at a time when many who claim to be Christians are Christ-less Christians.

> —The Anglican Bishop of Jerusalem, March 20, 2003

[We] raise our voice with His Holiness, John Paul II, to say that war is a defeat for humanity.

> —Evangelical Lutheran Church of the Middle East, March 25, 2003

We condemn this unjustified war, which has no international legitimacy . . . those engaged will bear a tremendous responsibility in front of God, the people and history.

> —The Jordanian Christian Council, April 14, 2003

As Evangelicals, Protestants, Anglicans and Christians we speak out against the war and say, "Not in our name."

> —Evangelicals from Mexico, Argentina and Peru, April 2, 2003

Churches around the world condemned this war as immoral.

—Middle East Council of Churches, March 21, 2003

[The] US-led war of aggression has no moral justification. It goes against the grain of the Christian tenet of justice and the right of sovereign nations to chart their future.

—The National Council of Churches in the Philippines, March 20, 2003

No to war! War is . . . always a defeat for humanity. International law, honest dialogue, solidarity between States, the noble exercise of diplomacy: these are methods worthy of individuals and nations in resolving their differences.

—Pope John Paul II, January 13, 2003

We call upon the nations of the world to stop military preparations against Iraq, to prevent bloodshed of innocent people. We plead with the God "to guide the feet into the way of peace" (Lk. 1:79) and to protect the biblical earth of Iraq against the fire of war.

—Russian Orthodox Church, March 17, 2003

It is therefore with the most profound sorrow that we view what has come to pass—a decision for war which has not even been put to the vote at the Security Council because its proponents had been unable to convince that Council's members of their case.

—The Church of Scotland, March 19, 2003

The Council . . . condemns this act as an immoral, illegal and ill advised venture which will only bring untold suffering and hardship on the ordinary civilians.

>—The National Christian Council of Sri Lanka,
> March 26, 2003

We beseech [the political leadership of the U.S.] to convert your hearts; to listen to the voices of your churches . . . to change direction; to look to the consensus of the nations, returning to the point where you abandoned them, and aim to contribute to the renewal and building of a multilateral, global foundation of governance with justice, and thus, stability.

>—The Waldensian Reformed Church of Italy,
> March 23, 2003

For some time, there has been present among some Christians, the theory of the "just war." It is a theory that searches for a moral justification of war. If the criteria of proportionality and immunity are important for a "just war" then it is difficult, if not impossible, to find any Christian or moral justification for the destruction of non-combatants. We stand aghast at the devastation wrought on the historic cities of Iraq by cruise missiles and smart bombs.

>—The Anglican Church in the Province of the
> West Indies, April 4, 2003

The Council therefore calls upon the United States, the United Kingdom and their supporters to end all hostilities in order to avoid the looming catastrophe that can only be the eventual outcome of this conflict.

>—World Methodist Council, March 28, 2003

> We condemn unreservedly this war of aggression, and we
> condemn the unilateral and imperial mentality that lies be-
> hind it. No nation, however powerful, may act on the world
> stage simply as it pleases. . . . We remind President George
> W. Bush and his administration that the gospel choice is to
> be for or against Christ.
>
> —World Alliance of Reformed Churches,
> March 20, 2003

And there are many more documents and statements posted by churches, denominational leaders, and Christian organizations around the globe. Nonetheless, the patriot preachers and the court prophets, that is, the white evangelical leaders in the United States whose sermons, articles, press releases, and media appearances generated near unanimous support from the evangelical congregations for the American invasion, paid little attention to the outcries of their brothers and sisters around the world. Against the backdrop of the war effort's near unanimous condemnation by the global and ecumenical church, the American evangelical elites and their congregations worked hard to align themselves with the thrilling mandates of the godly president.[24]

These years have been transformative in the religious history of the United States. It is arguably the moment when American evangelicalism ran aground. One thing is certain: Our hope for renewal depends on the willingness to reach out to these brothers and sisters abroad, and this starts with reaffirming our global interdependence as citizens in the kingdom of God. Our cry for help must decisively reshape the way we think about our life in the global Christian community. There are some signs of hope. The involvement of evangelical Christians in campaigns to address world hunger and to fortify resources in response to the global AIDS crisis is heartening. *Christianity Today*'s criticisms of the immoral torture and detention practices of the U.S. military, enumerated eloquently by Professor David Gushee, are symbolically powerful moments.[25] The emerging environmental consciousness among some evangelical leaders and laity signals a more holistic social mission. Even so, these encouraging trends, if not conditioned by clear and public confession of our support of the immoral and catastrophic war in Iraq and our complicity in the humiliation of word, will lack coherence and a vital center. Perhaps our willingness to free the gospel from political captivity requires not only repentance but reformation as well. In his essay "Protestantism without Reformation," written during his 1930 Sloan Fellowship at Union Theological Seminary in New York, Bonhoeffer noted that white Christians in the United States have never experienced a Reformation moment, a time when the churches were forced to stand fully on the truthfulness of the word, and, as a result, our priviledge encourages us to act as if we can have the gospel and everything else.

We have before us, however, an opportunity to reaffirm the oneness we share in Christ, which links us in a deeper stream to the human family, and to life. The body of Christ, exquisitely diverse and varied, teaches us that the gospel is not our own possession, that Christians must pass a global test. "Sing to the Lord a new song," exclaimed the prophet Isaiah, "his praise from the end of the earth" (42:10). Perhaps God will bring reformation out of our corruption.

Chapter Nine

FAITH AS MAKING SPACE FOR GOD'S TRUTH IN THE WORLD

A RE CHRISTIANS STILL of any use? If so, how should we now live after this time of accommodation and propaganda?

What we will need is not geniuses, or cynics, or misanthropes, or clever tacticians, but plain, honest, straightforward men and women," Bonhoeffer wrote in an essay entitled "After Ten Years: A Reckoning Made at New Year 1943."[1] Less than six months later, he was arrested on charges of "subversion of the armed forces." Bonhoeffer had become an active member of the German resistance, having grown disillusioned with the Confessing Church movement, and he now worked closely with humanists and atheists, whose concerns were broader than ecclesial reform. The Confessing Church movement had failed to dismantle the nazified German Evangelical Church or even to directly challenge the tyranny of the Führer.[2] But the close attention that Bonhoeffer's comrades in the political resistance gave to the moral imperatives of the day—concern for humanity, justice, and toleration—inspired Bonhoeffer to think more critically about the ways the Christian faith sometimes promotes withdrawal from the world and acquiescence to its brutalities. In the process, he came to a new appreciation of "good people" and "the beatification of those who are persecuted for the sake of a just cause."[3]

A worldly faith was now what the times required, if it required any faith at all; a worldly faith calling people to become passionately and irrepressibly human, lacking deviousness and deception, willing to admit mistakes and to follow the way of the cross into the complexities and anguishes of the day. "The Christian . . . has no last line of escape available from earthly tasks and difficulties into the eternal," Bonhoeffer wrote in prison, "but, like Christ himself ('My God, why hast thou forsaken me?'), he must drink the earthly cup to the dregs, and only in his doing so is the crucified and risen Lord with him, and he crucified and risen with Christ."[4]

What do we need in the American churches after this period of compromise and equivocation? "Are *we* still of any use?"[5]

We too need plain, honest, straightforward men and women. Above all, we will need to be known as people of truth, as people who show the world what it means to live in truth. We might even imagine faith as the art of making space for God's truth in the world. If Christians are to live according to a single mark in these late days, then, I say, let that mark be truth.

I have mentioned this before, but it bears repeating: I am struck by the absence of resistance, dissent, and critical judgment in the moral repertoire of contemporary evangelicals. These disciplines—and let us call them disciplines—are rarely intoned in our sermons, publications, and seminaries, and when they are, they are most commonly regarded as manifestations of pride. Evangelicals are quick to admonish unity when there is a whiff of disagreement in the air. Dissent must be quashed for the sake of harmonious ideals, which we consider spiritual virtues. But perhaps the situation only masks our swift retreat from the costs of discipleship, fueled by an inferiority complex, which plagues us even after winning the White House. We are failing to raise up a generation of Christian critics at a time when dissent should be a vital part of confessing Jesus Christ as Lord.[6]

Our dissent on dissent may be explained in part by a lack of intellectual curiosity. But the problem lies deeper, as we have seen. White evangelicals in the United States have never had to live solely on the truth of God, and we have made decisions about the shape of our economy, society, and political culture on the premise that we can have God and all the other things, or at least lots of other things, the shiny, happy things that inspire our devotion, without worries. While these decisions have yielded pleasures unprecedented in history, they have also helped form a religious environment that subjects any man or woman who seeks to live on the basis of truth to a slow and certain obliteration.

When "truth is fallen in the streets," as we read in the book of Isaiah, justice is "turned away backward" and "equity cannot enter." The Hebrew Bible teaches that the end of truth is the breeding ground of injustice. "The way of peace they know not; and there is no justice in their goings" (Isa. 59:8 ASV). We read that those who deceive "are following a crooked path and whoever enters this path will find no knowledge of peace" (Isa. 59:8 ASV). A nation that has transgressed and lied—not only against the Lord but against each other—will never know the shalom of God. "We have neither peace within nor peace without," Martin Luther King Jr. said in the final year of his life. "Everywhere paralyzing fears harrow people by day and haunt them by night. Our world is sick with war."[7] Conversely, the God who loves justice and despises injustice is the God served and worshipped in truth.

Faith makes space for the truth of God in the world. For this reason, the followers of Jesus must be marked by a wholehearted commitment to truth. In their essential book, *Terrorism and the War in Iraq: A Christian Word from Latin America,* the Argentinean evangelical theologian René Padilla and Wheaton College professor Lindy Scott wrote that Christian commitment "means more than just refraining from communicating falsehoods. It also means correcting falsehoods, even when that action is not convenient to your cause."[8] They continue: "The fact that key members of the Bush administration perpetuated the alleged, but false, connection between Saddam Hussein and the terrorist attacks of September 11 orchestrated by Al Qaeda and that they voluntarily communicated nothing to correct that misunderstanding by 70% of the United States population reveals a serious lack of integrity in our highest government officials."[9]

In THE SEVENTEENTH CHAPTER of the Gospel of John, Jesus prays in the hours before his arrest that the Father would protect the children of God; he prays that they all might be one. This is not a unity forged through uniformity and sameness but one gained through obedience and suffering. "I have given them your word; and the world has hated them because they do not belong to the world, just as I do not belong to the world. I am not asking that you take them out of the world, but I ask you to protect them from the evil one" (17:14).

Jesus prays that his followers will be sanctified "in the truth" for God's word is truth. "The word is thy truth." The children of

Jesus shall remain in the world: We do not presume to roam freely over history, to inhabit a land of precepts without footprints. But the truth in which Christians live in this world is "not of the world." Philosophers and wise men have searched for truth and constructed elaborate systems of thought, but now the truth has appeared in Jesus. "The word is *thy truth*." The world must then be understood on the basis of the truth of God. This does not mean that the world lacks truth, but that the truth of the world is found in God. So Jesus prays, "Sanctify them in thy truth."

The word "sanctify" and its derivative "sanctification" may resonate fretfully for some evangelical readers. Sanctification pertains to the expectation to become "holy" and "sanctified," hinting at the prospects of perfectionism. Evangelicals in the churches of my childhood believed that the pursuit of certain moral values was required in order to grow in Christ and advance in holiness. If we abstained from alcohol, dance, card-playing, sexual immorality, and other vices, and if we gave ourselves to Bible study, prayer, and soul-winning, we were on the right track toward godliness; we were being sanctified. The very idea of "growing in Christ" promised a time when we might be fully Christlike, which of course never happened, and which in turn filled us with shame. In the Gospel of John, however, Jesus speaks of the evangelical mission as a life of learning to live in truth and speak the truth, more as a habitation than an endpoint.

Gifted with the word of truth, the disciples of Jesus are then "sent into the world." As the Father sent the Son into the far country of the world to return the lost sheep to their home, so Jesus is sending his disciples into the world to proclaim the truth of God to the world. Put this way: Jesus commissions us with the mission of living in truth in the world. Jesus entrusts us with the truth. This is a venture full of risk and uncertainty. Sending his children into the world to show the world the unity of truth, to proclaim and to represent truth in its unsettling and yet creative and restorative power. Jesus' instruction is offered as a gift and not intended as a burden. God's unbounded love is expressed in the promise to guard and bless those who live honestly in face of deception and artifice. But Jesus takes the risk of entrusting his children with truth, for in this way, "the love with which You loved me may be in them, and I in them." When the children of God retreat from their commitment to truth, they become accomplices in the world's assault on the word.

"I in them, and You in Me; that they may be made perfect in one, and that the world may know that You have sent Me, and have loved them as You have loved Me."

Shortly after his prayer in the Garden of Gethsemane, Jesus is betrayed, arrested, and led to his crucifixion. God's love for the lost sheep endures all the way to the cross, and there it becomes the peace of the world. Jesus' own final and complete acceptance of a brutal death reveals a world beyond fear, violence, and dread, the world whose truth is peace. "Peace be with you," Jesus says in the days following the resurrection.

Christians must speak the truth so that the world may believe that God has sent them. And the truth spoken is not only the truth about God—that God so loved the world—but it is truth as such, plain, ordinary, and hard as rock. "'Falsehood' is the destruction of, and hostility to, reality as it is in God." Bonhoeffer says, "To be simple is to fix one's eye solely on the simple truth of God at a time when all concepts are being confused, distorted and turned upside-down."[10]

Christians must then stand on the solid ground of truth. God spoke, and the word of God created the heavens and earth. "All things come into being through him." If Christians are people of truth, then we are also marked as disciples of Jesus Christ by our respect for language and meaning. Heresy these days is rarely a mad assault on the holy; it is rather the accumulation of pious phrases adjusted for personal comfort and needs, though this banality of heresy has surely led to destruction, chaos, and plagues of hopelessness.

In the beginning was the Word, and the Word was with God, and the Word was God. A testimony of the Word begins with truth. The word of God is a light that illuminates the unjust and ugly spaces of the world. Christians must follow this light with courage and sobriety. We must say with Saint Augustine, "I depend on you to enable me to speak the truth."[11]

IN THE POSTMODERN WHITE HOUSE, truth recedes behind image and spin; reality is built on the infinite deferral of fact. Evangelicals have never been fans of the postmodern paradigm. Forums on the demise of objective truth are seen throughout our subculture, in our colleges, Web sites, periodicals, and study centers. Hundreds of books by evangelical writers have been written that survey with varying degrees of opprobrium and outrage the corrosive effects of postmodern thought. "Civilization is shaped by ideas," wrote one evangelical apologist, "and the loss of truth as the fixed reference point by which civilization can be guided leads to moral chaos."[12] It is disquieting then that the churches have applauded so gleefully the postmodern president.

Perhaps now is the time, after all the compromises and equivocations, to recall the wisdom attributed to Martin Luther, that it would be better to vote for a wise Turk than a pious fool, and, more important, that it might be sufficient for the emperor to possess reason.[13] Perhaps we should hereafter pledge to vote on the basis of rational, intelligible, and biblically responsible criteria, and, further, to affirm the role of natural reason and common grace in thinking about our moral and civic habits before the social order falls fully victim to our distinctive vocabularies. I agree with the biblical scholar and Anglican bishop N. T. Wright that the church "must recover both its nerve and its faith in God-given reason, not as an independent source of authority but as the tool for thinking clearly, for working through contemporary challenges to truth (the idea of truth itself, as well as its content) and questions about behaviour and discovering fresh ways forward."[14]

Look what the evangelical empire has produced: a world bereft of moral accountability, intellectual curiosity, trustworthiness, and honesty. The language games we have played, along with the breezy hook-up of meaning, will be the legacy of the last remaining superpower to the coming generations. The postmodern White House is an incubator of epistemological terror: the deconstructions of war, the torture chambers, the forgotten populations of New Orleans, the neglect of the earth, the webs of duplicity and deception. At least, postmodernism has been finally exposed as brute power, cosmic entitlement, and boutique mysticism. Truth is infinitely adaptable to shifting interests, slain with a shrug and a grin.[15]

In his book *FAITH AND VIOLENCE*, Thomas Merton urged Christians to realize that our calling does not make us superior to other people. We are not called to be masters of meaning, to colonize

the truth and make it our possession. Christians must rather learn
to participate in God's created order and thus to link arms with all
those who care about the human condition and the created order.
Our job as Christians is "to struggle along with everybody else
and collaborate with them in the difficult, frustrating task of seeking a solution to common problems, which are entirely new and
strange to us all."[16] This illuminates both our hope and our discipline: to speak with "the humility that is appropriate to our limited vision," and by speaking to take part in shared human
struggle. "One must not only preach a sermon with his voice,"
Martin Luther King Jr. said. "He must preach it with his life."[17]
Abiding with Christ, we learn to relinquish our claims on God
and to see that shared struggle is the place where proper humility
is forever nourished.

Jesus said: "Peace I leave with you; my peace I give to you.
I do not give to you as the world gives. Do not let your hearts be
troubled, and do not let them be afraid" (John 14:27).

NOTES

Introduction

1. Dietrich Bonhoeffer, *Letters and Papers from Prison* (New York: Macmillan, 1972), 300.
2. Ibid., 300.
3. Dietrich Bonhoeffer cited in Nelson, F. Burton, "The Relationship of Jean Lasserre to Dietrich Bonhoeffer's Peace Concerns in the Struggle of Church and Culture," *Union Seminary Quarterly Review*, vol. 8, 1–2 (1985): 78.
4. Deborah Caldwell, "Did God Intervene? Evangelicals are crediting God with securing re-election victory for George W. Bush," Beliefnet, www.beliefnet.com/story/123/story_12365_1.html
5. Sam Harris, *The End of Faith: Religion, Terror, and the Future of Reason* (New York: W. W. Norton & and Company, 2004).
6. The Pew Charitable Trusts, "War Concerns Grow but Support Remains Steadfast," http://www.pewtrusts.com, April 3, 2003.
7. Karl Barth, *Against the Stream: Shorter Post-War Writings* (New York: Philosophical Library, 1954), 185. To say that Jesus comes to us from

the far country of God may mean placing oneself into a wholly new place in relation to faith. What could be stranger than God appearing on a cross, as a tortured enemy of the state?

8. Bonhoeffer, *Letters and Papers from Prison*, 161.

9. Karl Barth, *The Word of God and the Word of Man*, trans. Douglas Horton (Gloucester, MA: Peter Smith, 1978), 297.

10. *The Nicene Creed.*

11. *The Concise Oxford Dictionary of Current English* (Oxford: Clarendon Press, 1911).

12. Mark Dowd, "A Bush That Burns," *New Statesman*, November 1, 2004.

13. See my article, "In Defense of a Self: The Theological Search for a Postmodern Identity," *Scottish Journal of Theology* 55 (2002): 253–82, for a detailed discussion of Christian theology and self-affirmation.

14. Barth, *Against the Stream*, 72.

15. Cited C. René Padilla and Lindy Scott, *Terrorism and the War in Iraq: A Christian Word from Latin America* (Buenos Aires: Kairos Ediciones, 2004), 14.

16. Ibid.

17. Jerry Falwell, "Falwell Confidential," Jerry Falwell Ministries, http://www.falwell.com.

18. The term comes from Jacques Ellul, *The Humiliation of the Word*, trans. Joyce Main Hanks (Grand Rapids, MI: Eerdmans, 1985).

19. Dietrich Bonhoeffer, *Life Together*, trans. John W. Doberstein (San Francisco: Harper & Row, 1954), 80. The sense of Bonhoeffer's meditation is that although we cannot be silent forever, we must learn to be silent when silence is required. "If we have learned to be silent before the Word, we shall also learn to manage our silence and our speech during the day" (80).

20. Bonhoeffer, *Letters and Papers from Prison*, 16.

21. Barth, *The Word of God and the Word of Man*, 294.

22. Barth, *Against the Stream*, 69.

23. Bonhoeffer, *Letters and Papers from Prison*, 16. Jean Lasserre, the French evangelical pastor and peace activist, with whom Bonhoeffer

became friends during their year together at Union Theological Seminary in 1930–1931, spoke eloquently with the American theologian F. Burton Nelson in a 1977 interview on the new global identity of the Christian: "[What] is absolutely awful and unacceptable in war is that Christians are compelled to forget their Christian faith and Christian belonging to the Church, to the universal, to the real Church" (F. Burton Nelson, "The Relationship of Jean Lasserre to Dietrich Bonhoeffer's Peace Concerns in the Struggle of Church and Culture," *Union Seminary Quarterly Review* vol. 8, 1–2 [1985]: 76).

Chapter One

1. Francis Schaeffer, *A Christian Manifesto*, vol. 5 of *The Complete Works of Francis A. Schaeffer* (New York: Crossway Books, 1982), 459.
2. Marvin Olasky, "Francis Schaeffer's political legacy," www.townhall.com/columnists/MarvinOlasky/2005/03/03/francis_schaeffers_political_legacy.
3. Ibid.
4. See Michael S. Hamilton's helpful article, "The Dissatisfaction of Francis Schaeffer," *Christianity Today*, March 3, 1997. Hamilton writes, "This small, intense man from the Swiss mountains delivered a message unlike any heard in evangelical circles in the mid-1960s. At Wheaton College (where he delivered the lectures that became his first book, *The God Who Is There*), students were fighting to show films like *Bambi*, while Francis was talking about the films of Bergman and Fellini. Administrators were censoring existential themes out of student publications, while Francis was discussing Camus, Sartre, and Heidegger. He quoted Dylan Thomas, knew the artwork of Salvador Dali, listened to the music of the Beatles and John Cage . . . Francis Schaeffer tore down the gospel curtain that had separated evangelicals from contemporary cultural expression, giving Christian object lessons in how to interpret sculpture, music painting, and literature as philosophical statements of the modern mind."

5. Schaeffer, *Christian Manifesto*, 458.
6. Ibid.
7. Cited on Langham Partnership International, www.johnstott.org.
8. Lausanne Committee for World Evangelism: Lausanne 1974; www .lausanne.org.
9. "The Lausanne Covenant," Lausanne 1974, www.lausanne.org/Brix? pageID=12891. All following quotations from the Covenant are taken from this source.
10. Francis Schaeffer, *The Great Evangelical Disaster* (New York: Crossway Books, 1984), 76.
11. John Stott, *Christian Counter-Culture: The Message of the Sermon on the Mount* (Downers Grove, IL: InterVarsity Press, 1978), 54.
12. Ibid., 54.
13. Ibid., 19.
14. "The Lausanne Covenant."
15. R. H. Mounce, "Gospel," in *Evangelical Dictionary of Theology*, edited by Walter Elwell (Grand Rapids, MI: Baker Book House, 1984), 472.
16. Ibid.
17. See Miroslav Volf's book by the same name, *Free of Charge: Giving and Forgiving in a Culture Stripped of Grace* (Grand Rapids, MI: Zondervan, 2005).
18. Augustine, "Sermons on New Testament Lessons," *The Works of St. Augustine*, ed. Philip Schaff (Peabody, MA: Philip Schaff, 1999), 425.
19. Jack Kerouac, *On the Road* (New York: Penguin, 1976), 5.
20. The term comes from Nicholas Wolterstorff's book *Reason within the Bounds of Religion Alone* (Grand Rapids, MI: Eerdmans, 1976).
21. Dietrich Bonhoeffer, *The Cost of Discipleship*, trans. R. H. Fuller (New York: Macmillan, 1963), 116.
22. Wendy Murray Zoba, *Day of Reckoning: Columbine and the Search for America's Soul* (Grand Rapids, MI: Brazos Press, 2001), 89. See Misty Bernall, *She Said Yes* (Farmington, PA: Plough Publishing, 1999).
23. Bonhoeffer, *Letters and Papers from Prison*, 161.

Chapter Two

1. George W. Bush, cited in John C. McCollister, *God and the Oval Office* (Nashville, TN: W Publishing Group, 2005), 238.

2. See Deborah Caldwell, "Poised and Ready," Beliefnet, www. beliefnet .com/story/123/story_12365_1.html.

3. However, church leaders in South America were having none of it. In November 2003, Franklin Graham was scheduled to begin an evangelistic campaign in Argentina. The Kairos Community objected strongly, stating in a public letter that the younger Graham's presence would create "an ethical problem of great magnitude, if we keep in mind that Franklin Graham is a religious advisor to George W. Bush, and is frankly offensive, among other reasons, for the explicit support that the preacher gave to the invasion of Iraq by the United States." The Argentinean Christians continued: "While almost the entire world, including many Argentine men and women, perceive the bellicose actions of the governments of George Bush and Tony Blair as a criminal act, how can we Argentine evangelicals give a welcome to someone who has contributed to the utilization of our faith to justify such an act?" (cited in Padilla and Scott, *Terrorism and the War in Iraq*, 2).

4. Marvin Olasky, "Compassionate War?" *World Magazine*, April 19, 2003.

5. Jack Graham, "Comments on War in Iraq," March 20, 2003, http://www .prestonwood.org.

6. Paul Crouch, "TBN Newsletter: Iraq—Here We Come!" Trinity Broadcast Network, http://www.tbn.org/about/newsletter/index.php/378.html.

7. Ibid.

8. Richard B. Hays, *The Moral Vision of the New Testament: A Contemporary Introduction to New Testament Ethics* (San Francisco: HarperSanFrancisco, 1996), 337.

9. Karl Barth, *The Humanity of God* (Richmond, VA: John Knox Press, 1960), 28.

10. James Kennedy and Jim Nelson Black, *Character and Destiny: A Nation in Search of Its Soul* (Grand Rapids, MI: Zondervan, 1994), 91.

11. Ibid., 91.

12. Barth, *The Humanity of God,* 19.

13. Ibid.

14. Ibid.

15. Bonhoeffer, *Letters and Papers from Prison,* 16.

16. Paul Nelson Walker, *Sermons for Christ Church* (Charlottesville, VA: 2001), 107.

17. John H. Leith, "The Creeds and Their Role in the Church," in *Creeds of the Churches: A Reader in Christian Doctrine from the Bible to the Present,* 3rd ed. (Louisville: Westminster John Knox Press, 1982), 1.

18. Robert Sokolowski, *The God of Faith and Reason: Foundations of Christian Theology* (Notre Dame, IN: University of Notre Dame Press, 1982), 33–34.

19. Ibid.

20. Eberhard Jungel, *God as the Mystery of the World* (Edinburgh: T&T Clark, 1999), 336ff.

21. See John De Gruchy, "Holy Beauty: A Reformed Perspective on Aesthetics within a World of Unjust Ugliness," The Project on Lived Theology, http://www.livedtheology.org/pdfs/deGruchy.pdf.

22. Eugene Robertson cited in *The Washington Post,* "Televangelist Calls for Chavez' Death," Tuesday, August 23, 2005.

23. *Washington Post,* August 25, 2005.

24. Jerry Falwell and Pat Robertson, "You Helped This Happen," Beliefnet, http://www.beliefnet.com/story/87/story_8770_1.html.

25. Robertson has said of Chavez, "You know, I don't know about this doctrine of assassination, but if he thinks we're trying to assassinate him, I think that we really ought to go ahead and do it. It's a whole lot cheaper than starting a war." He continued, "We have the ability to take him out, and I think the time has come that we exercise that ability. We don't need another $200 billion war to get rid of one, you know, strong-arm dictator. It's a whole lot easier to have some of the covert operatives do the job and then get it over with" (CNN, August 25, 2005).

26. Eugene Robertson, "After Castro, Chavez," *Washington Post*, August 26, 2005.

27. "Editorial: Judgment Malfunction," *New York Times*, August 25, 2005.

28. Although the Southern Baptist Convention supported the war, the Baptist World Alliance, the association of international Baptists which includes some individual Southern Baptists, condemned the American invasion as "a great sin," declaring that "war is always a failure of humanity to achieve the will of God for peace" (cited in Padilla and Scott, *Terrorism and the War in Iraq*, 15).

29. "The Lausanne Covenant."

Chapter Three

1. Amy Sullivan, "Why W. Doesn't Go to Church," *The New Republic*, October, 11, 2004.

2. Steven Strang, "The Faith of George W. Bush," *Charisma*, October, 2003; "An Inaugural Moment," *Charisma*, March, 2005.

3. See Joan Didion, "Mr. Bush and the Divine," *New York Review of Books*, November 6, 2003. See also Kevin Philips, *American Theocracy: The Peril and Politics of Radical Religion, Oil and Borrowed Money in the 21st Century* (New York: Viking, 2006).

4. Alan Jacobs, "Apocalyptic President?" *The Boston Globe*, April 4, 2004.

5. Marshall Frady, *Billy Graham: A Parable of American Righteousness* (New York: Little, Brown, 1979), 212.

6. Billy Graham, *Just As I Am: The Autobiography of Billy Graham* (San Francisco: Harper/Zondervan, 1997), 724.

7. Charles Marsh, "One, Two, Three, What Are We Praying For?" *Baltimore Sun*, February 2, 1991.

8. Aikman borrowed the C. S. Lewis term from Tim Goeglein, the director of the White House Office of Public Liaison and the president's intermediary with Christian organizations, although Aikman did not mention Goeglein by name in his book. Goeglein offered this description to a *Washington Post* reporter while making the case that the president,

as in Lewis's book by the same name, is a Christian who "believes in the essentials and has no interest in the inessentials." Alan Cooperman, *Washington Post*, Thursday, September 16, 2004.

9. See my book, *The Last Days: A Son's Story of Sin and Segregation at the Dawn of a New South* (New York: Basic Books, 2001), and see also Charles Marsh, "Among the Jesus Freaks," www.killingthebuddha .com/confession/among_jesus_freaks.htm.

10. David Aikman, *A Man of Faith: The Spiritual Journey of George W. Bush* (Nashville, TN: W Publishing Group, 2004), 74.

11. Arthur Blessitt, "The Day I Prayed with George W. Bush to Receive Jesus!" www.blessitt.com/bush.html.

12. Aikman, *A Man of Faith*, 74.

13. Ibid., 72.

14. Jim Sales, another oilman from Midland, Texas, was the only eyewitness to the conversion prayer, and he has confirmed that "what happened is precisely as recorded in Blessitt's testimony" (Stephen Mansfield, *The Faith of George W. Bush* [New York: Tarcher, 2003], 65).

15. George W. Bush cited in Aikman, *A Man of Faith*, 74.

16. Aikman, *A Man of Faith*, 74.

17. Tony Carnes, "The spiritual journey of George W. Bush starts in hardscrabble west Texas. Will the White House be his next stop?" *Christianity Today*, posted at www.christianitytoday.com, September 9, 2000. The story is repeated by Mansfield, *The Faith of George W. Bush*, 68.

18. George W. Bush, *A Charge to Keep: My Journey to the White House* (New York: William Morrow, 1999), 136.

19. Ibid.

20. Bush cited in Aikman, *A Man of Faith*, 77.

21. Bush, *A Charge to Keep*, 136.

22. James Robison cited in Mansfield, *The Faith of George W. Bush*, 76.

23. David Aikman, *A Man of Faith*, 79.

24. George W. Bush, "Interview: We Are All Sinners," www.beliefnet .com/story/47/story_4703_1.html.

25. C. S. Lewis, *Mere Christianity* (New York: Macmillan Publishing, 1952), 56.

26. Cited in Aikman, *A Man of Faith*, 74.

27. Ibid., 80.

28. Ibid.

29. Irenaeus, *Against Heresies*, ed. Alexander Roberts and James Donaldson (Grand Rapids, MI: Eerdmans, 1989), 443.

30. Irenaeus cited in J. N. D. Kelly, *Early Christian Doctrines* (New York: Harper, 1960), 173.

31. Bonhoeffer, *Letters and Papers from Prison*, 170. Irenaeus's meditations on the cosmic benefits of Christ, as Bonhoeffer also notes, are based on Saint Paul's remarks to the Ephesians: "In him we have redemption through his blood, the forgiveness of our trespasses, according to the riches of his grace that he lavished on us. With all wisdom and insight he has made known to us the mystery of his will, according to his good pleasure that he set forth in Christ, as a plan for the fullness of time, to gather up all things in him, things in heaven and things on earth" (Eph. 1:7–10).

32. Bonhoeffer, *Letters and Papers from Prison*, 170.

33. *Evangelical Dictionary of Theology*, ed. Walter A. Elwell (Grand Rapids, MI: Baker Book House, 1984), 508.

Chapter Four

1. Martin Luther, "The Pagan Servitude of the Church," in *Martin Luther: A Selection from His Writings*, ed. John Dillenberger (New York: Anchor, 1968), 250.

2. Christopher Rowland, *Radical Christianity: A Reading of Recovery* (Cambridge and Oxford, England: Polity Press, 1988), 161.

3. Will D. Campbell, "An Oral History with Will D. Campbell," by Orley B. Caudill, University of Southern Mississippi Libraries, The University of Southern Mississippi, Center for Oral History and Cultural Heritage.

4. John Dittmer, *Local People: The Struggle for Civil Rights in Mississippi* (Urbana, IL: University of Illinois Press, 1994), 63.

5. Will D. Campbell, conversation with the author.

6. Will D. Campbell, *Race and the Renewal of the Church* (Philadelphia: The Westminster Press, 1962), 8.

7. Ibid., 10.

8. Will D. Campbell, conversation with the author.

9. Barbara Ritter Dailey, "Will D. Campbell," in *Twentieth-Century Shapers of American Popular Religion*, ed. Charles H. Lippy (Westport, CT: Greenwood Press, 1989), 89.

10. Campbell in "An Oral History with Will D. Campbell."

11. Will D. Campbell, "The World of the Redneck," *Christianity and Crisis*, May 27, 1974, 118.

12. Will D. Campbell, *Brother to a Dragonfly* (New York: Continuum, 1977), 230.

13. Will D. Campbell, conversation with the author.

14. Will D. Campbell, correspondence to Walker Percy, September 2, 1965. University of Southern Mississippi Libraries, The University of Southern Mississippi.

15. For more on the dark career of Sam Bowers, see my book, *God's Long Summer: Stories of Faith and Civil Rights* (Princeton: Princeton University Press, 1997), chapter 2; see also the article, "Rendezvous with the Wizard," *Oxford American*, Fall, 1997.

16. Friedrich Nietzsche, *The Anti-Christ*, trans. Anthony M. Ludovic (New York: Prometheus Books), 200.

17. Michael Budde, *The (Magic) Kingdom of God: Christianity and Global Industries* (Boulder, CO: Westview Press, 1997), 2.

18. Budde, *The (Magic) Kingdom of God*, 2.

19. *St. Mathetes Epistle to Diognetus, The Ante-Nicene Fathers: Translations of the Writings of the Fathers down to A.D. 325*, ed. Alexander Roberts and James Donaldson (Peabody, MA: Henrickson, 1980), 26. Diogn. 5:4.

20. *Apostolic Fathers* (Lightfoot & Harmer, 1891 translation), Diogn. 5: 2–16.

Chapter Five

1. Reinhold Niebuhr, *Radical Religion*, 4 (Spring, 1937): 2–3. Cited in D. R. Davies, *Reinhold Niebuhr: Prophet from America* (New York: Macmillan, 1948), 79.
2. Harvey Cox, *The Secular City* (New York: Macmillan, 1965), 14.
3. Ibid., 235.
4. Karl Barth, *Church Dogmatics*, vol. I, pt. 1 (Edinburgh: T&T Clark, 1975), 3.
5. John Leith, *Creeds of the Churches*, 1. Following references will be noted parenthetically.
6. Karl Barth, "The First Commandment as the Axiom of Theology," in *The Way of Theology in Karl Barth: Essays and Comments* (Allison Park, PA: Pickwick Publication, 1986), 64.
7. Hans Frei, *Types of Christian Theology*, ed. George Hunsinger and William C. Placher (New Haven, CT: Yale University Press, 1992), 159.
8. Karl Barth, *The Epistle to the Romans*, trans. Edwyn C. Hoskyns (New York: Oxford University Press), 28.
9. Barth, "The First Commandment," 71.
10. Falwell cited in Warren L. Vinz, *Pulpit Politics: Faces of American Protestant Nationalism in the Twentieth Century* (Albany, NY: State University of New York Press, 1997), 171.
11. Jim Wallis, *God's Politics: Why the Right Gets It Wrong and the Left Doesn't Get It* (San Francisco: HarperSanFrancisco, 2005), xiv–xv.
12. See Wallis, "Class Warfare," *Sojourners*, Sept.–Oct. 2003.
13. Ibid., 30.
14. He also claimed this for the ideas of world and the self, but my purpose is not to provide a summary of Kant's epistemology. That can be

found in my 500-page doctoral dissertation, chapter four, located somewhere on the bottom floor of Alderman Library at the University of Virginia.

15. Friedrich Schleiermacher, *On Religion: Speeches to Its Cultured Despisers* (New York: Harper, 1958), 39.

16. Ibid., 43.

17. Barth, *The Humanity of God*, 25.

18. Ibid., 26.

19. John Calvin, *Institutes of the Christian Religion*, vol. I, ed. John T. McNeill (Philadelphia: The Westminster Press, 1960), 686.

20. Alan Davies, *Infected Christianity: A Study of Modern Racism* (Kingston, ON: McGill-Queen's University Press, 1988), 32.

21. Ibid.

22. Ibid., 38.

23. Euclid B. Rogers, *Atonement* (Springfield, IL: The Springfield Library Publishing Company, 1908), 24.

24. Barth, *Church Dogmatics*, II/1:275.

25. Ibid., 275–77.

26. Ibid.

27. Alexander Schmemann, *For the Life of the World* (Crestwood, NY: St. Vladimir's Seminary Press, 1998), 29.

28. See www.iraqbodycount.net. These were the numbers the site was publishing on December 23, 2006.

29. David Brown, "Study Claims Iraq's 'Excess' Death Toll Has Reached 655,000," Wednesday, October 11, 2006, *The Washington Post*.

Chapter Six

1. Thomas Merton cited in Kenneth Leech, *Experiencing God: Theology as Spirituality* (San Francisco: Harper & Row, 1985), 129. 1 Kings 19:3–9.

2. Shepherd cited in Leech, *Experiencing God*, 130.

3. Athanasius, *The Life of Antony and the Letter to Marcellinus*, translated and edited by Robert C. Gregg (New York: Paulist Press, 1979), 42. Following references will be noted parenthetically.

4. For more on the women of the early monastic movement, see Margot H. King, "The Desert Mothers: A Survey of the Feminine Anchoretic Tradition in Western Europe," Peregrina Publishing, www.peregrina.com /matrologia_latina/DesertMothers1.html; and Laura Swan, *The Forgotten Desert Mothers: Sayings, Lives, and Stories of Early Christian Women* (Mahwah, NJ: Paulist Press, 2001).

5. Athanasius, *Life of Antony*, 42.

6. Leech, *Experiencing God*, 130.

7. Num. 25:5–6; cited in *Life of Antony*, 65.

8. Athanasius, *Life of Antony*, 65.

9. Ibid., 68.

10. Leech, *Experiencing God*, 142.

11. Ibid.

12. As the classic of medieval mysticism, *The Cloud of Unknowing*, later affirms: "A soul that is given wholly to contemplation . . . does everything it can to make all men as whole as itself." Cited in Leech, *Experiencing God*, 151.

13. Augustine, *Confessions*, trans. Henry Chadwick (New York: Oxford University Press, 1991), 265.

14. Ibid., 304.

15. Romano Guardini, *The Conversion of Augustine* (Westminster, MD: Newman Press, 1960), 94.

16. Augustine, *Confessions*, i, 2, in Guardini, *The Conversion of Augustine*, 93.

17. Guardini, *The Conversion of Augustine*, 94

18. Ibid., 93.

19. Augustine, *Confessions*, 265.

20. Ibid., 3.

21. John Calvin, *Institutes of the Christian Religion*, vol. I, 49. Following references will be noted parenthetically.

22. Victor Giraud cited in Emile Cailliet, *Pascal: The Emergence of Genius* (New York: Harper & Brothers, 1961), 132. A pamphlet found among Pascal's literary effects, *L'Écrit sur la conversion du pércheur*, contained many of the same lines as the parchment, but reads more directly as a confession of his belief in God, and as Victor Giraud says, an attempt to capture in language "a very precise personal experience."

23. Cailliet, *Pascal*, 136.

24. Walter Eichrodt, *Theology of the Old Testament*, cited in Donald W. McCullough, *The Trivialization of God: The Dangerous Illusion of a Manageable Deity* (Colorado Springs: Navpress, 1995), 79.

25. Pascal, *Pensées*, trans. W. F. Trotter (New York: The Modern Library, 1941), 314.

26. Ibid.

27. Thomas Merton, *The Intimate Merton: His Life from His Journals* (San Francisco: HarperSanFrancisco, 2001), 210.

28. Richard Land, cited on "Frontline: The Jesus Factor" PBS, www.pbs .org/wgbh/pages/frontline/shows/jesus/interviews/land.html. Land says further, "George W. Bush is standing squarely in the middle of American history and American tradition, and believing American exceptionalism . . . I believe that. I believe that the United States of America has a divinely given responsibility to hold up the flame of freedom, and whenever possible, to advance it."

29. Saint Thérèse of Lisieux, *Story of a Soul*, trans. John Clarke (Washington, DC: ICS Publications, 1977), 188.

30. Saint Thérèse of Lisieux, cited in the *New Jerusalem Bible: Saints Devotional Edition* (New York: Doubleday, 2002), 795.

31. Ibid.

32. Henri de Lubac, *The Discovery of God*, trans. Alexander Dru (Grand Rapids, MI: Eerdmans, 1956), 159.

33. Conversations with my colleague Charles Mathewes; see also Augustine, *City of God*, chapters 20 and 22.

34. Conversation with Charles Mathewes.

35. Barth, *The Word of God and the Word of Man*, 11–12. Following references will be noted parenthetically.

36. Barth makes this point in the later address, "Biblical Questions, Insights and Vistas," *The Word of God and the Word of Man*, 67.

37. Ibid., 67.

38. Ibid., 21.

39. The Danish philosopher and Christian existentialist Søren Kierkegaard, whom Barth was also reading at the time, wrote that "where all are Christians, the situation is this: to call oneself a Christian is the means whereby one secures oneself against all sorts of inconveniences and discomforts, and the means whereby one secures worldly goods, comforts, profits, etc." From "Attack upon Christendom," in *A Kierkegaard Anthology*, ed. Robert Bretall (Princeton: Princeton University Press, 1973), 437.

40. Barth, *The Word of God and the Word of Man*, 23.

41. Ibid., 25.

42. Ibid., 27.

43. Thomas Merton, *Raids on the Unspeakable* (New York: New Directions Publishing Corporation, 1966), 67. Following references will be noted parenthetically.

44. Ibid., 73.

45. Nicholas Lash, *Holiness, Speech and Silence: Reflections on the Question of God* (Cambridge, UK: Ashgate, 2004), 92.

Chapter Seven

1. "I once proposed, for the sake of provocation, that the church impose a thirty-year moratorium on all of its archetypal language. Were this to happen . . . the church would have to develop a new terminology." Paul Tillich, *On the Boundary: An Autobiographical Sketch* (London: Collins, 1967), 65.

2. Bonhoeffer, *Letters and Papers from Prison*, 300.

3. Rowan Williams, www.archbishopofcanterbury.org.

4. Dietrich Bonhoeffer, *Christ the Center*, trans. Edwin H. Robertson (New York: Harper & Row, 1978), 27.

5. Ibid., 62.

6. Thomas Merton, "Letter written to James H. Forest, February 21, 1966," in *The Hidden Ground of Love: The Letters of Thomas Merton on Religious Experience and Social Concerns* (New York: Farrar, Straus and Giroux, 1985).

7. Max Picard, *The World of Silence*, trans. Stanley Godwin (Wichita, KA: Eight Day Press, 2002 reprint; originally published 1948), 35.

8. David Elkind, *The Hurried Child: Growing Up Too Fast Too Soon* (New York: Perseus Books, 2001), xvi.

9. See Albert Raboteau's important essay, "American Christianity," *Boston Review* (April/May 2005).

10. Pascal, *Pensées*, section 136.

11. Bonhoeffer, *Life Together*, 79–80.

12. For theological purposes, it is important to emphasize that this unity is an asymmetrical one, inasmuch as the unity of God and the world is enabled and sustained by God's action alone. See my book *Reclaiming Dietrich Bonhoeffer: The Promise of His Theology* (New York: Oxford University Press, 1994), chapter 1.

13. Josef Pieper, *Leisure: The Basis of Culture*, trans. Gerald Malsbary (South Bend, IN: St. Augustine's Press, 1998), 100.

14. My friend, the writer and historian Lauren Winner, when lecturing on the spiritual disciplines, often tells the story of a Midrash on the Ten Commandments. Why, the rabbis ask, did God begin the Ten Commandments with the letter *alef*, a silent letter? The answer is that what was new at Sinai was not that God suddenly started talking to his people; what was new was that God first silenced the hum and buzz and chatter, so that his people could hear him.

15. What does the Lord require of Judah and Jerusalem in our time. "Wash yourselves; make yourselves clean; remove the evil of your doings from before my eyes . . . Seek justice" (Isa. 1:16). Seeking justice is also an

act of the whole self, but an act that brings the self to wholeness. "For ye shall go out with joy, and be led back with peace: the mountains and the hills before you shall burst forth into song; and all the trees of the fields shall clap their hands" (55:12).

16. Bonhoeffer, *Life Together*, 81.

17. See Nancy Muers, *Keeping God's Silence: Towards a Theological Ethics of Communication* (Cambridge, UK: Cambridge University Press, 2005), 22–38.

18. Dietrich Bonhoeffer, *Letters and Papers from Prison*, 391.

19. Christoph Blumhardt, *Action in Waiting* (Farmington, PA: The Plough Publishing House, 1998), 19.

20. See Alan E. Lewis, *Between the Cross and Resurrection: A Theology of Holy Saturday* (Grand Rapids, MI: Eerdmans, 2001), 218.

21. Karl Barth, *The Word of God and the Word of Man*.

22. Ellul, *The Humiliation of the Word*, 47.

23. Nancy Muers, *Keeping God's Silence*, 170.

24. The theologian Frits de Lange writes, "Speaking of God requires first of all silence and listening, prayerful listening. It receives power only when supported by doing justice. If Bonhoeffer defends a theology of the Word, it is a theology that does not limit itself to words alone." *Waiting for the Word: Dietrich Bonhoeffer on Speaking about God* (Grand Rapids, MI: Eerdmans, 1999), 37.

25. De Lange, *Waiting for the Word*, 35.

26. Richard Rorty, *Philosophy and Social Hope*, (New York: Penguin Books, 1999), 169–170.

27. Bonhoeffer, *Christ the Center*, 27.

28. Dietrich Bonhoeffer, "After Ten Years: A Reckoning Made at New Year 1943," from *Letters and Papers from Prison*, 3–17.

Chapter Eight

1. Tertullian, *Apology*, Chapter 28.

2. Saint Augustine: "This heavenly city, then, while it sojourns on earth, calls citizens out of all nations, and gathers together a society of pilgrims of all languages, not scrupling about diversities in the manners, laws, and institutions whereby earthly peace is secured and maintained, but recognizing that, however various these are, they all tend to one and the same end of earthly peace. It therefore is so far from rescinding and abolishing these diversities, that it even preserves and adopts them, so long only as no hindrance to the worship of the one supreme and true God is thus introduced" (*The City of God*, trans. Marcus Dods [New York: The Modern Library, 1950], Book XIX).

3. Philip Jenkins, *The Next Christendom: The Coming of Global Christianity* (New York: Oxford University Press, 2002), 18.

4. Ibid.

5. Importantly, one of the evangelical leaders who asked this question directly was Leighton Ford, the former vice president of the Billy Graham Evangelistic Association, who wrote in an open letter to "young Christian leaders": "We often forget that in the Middle East and the Arab countries there are not only Muslims and Jews, but fellow followers of Christ. How will a war affect them?" Ford concluded his letter by offering his hope that the United States continue to "keep the pressure on Saddam to disarm" while shifting its vast energies to "another war, one well worth fighting—the war against HIV-AIDS in southern Africa and much of Asia . . . War with Iraq will end many lives. War against AIDS will save tens of thousands of lives. So let's ask ourselves, and our leaders: which war is most worth fighting? There's still time to seek an alternative to war" (Leighton Ford, "A Letter from Leighton Ford to Young Christian Leaders," John Mark Ministries, http://jmm.aaa.net.au/articles/1607.htm).

6. As the African theologian John Mbiti observes, "The centers of the church's universality [are] no longer in Geneva, Rome, Athens, Paris,

London, New York, but Kinshasa, Buenos Aires, Addis Ababa, and Manila." John Mbiti cited in Jenkins, *The Next Christendom*, 2. Following references from *The Next Christendom* will be noted parenthetically.

7. Too often, statements about what "modern Christians believe" refer only to what "that ever-shrinking remnant of Western Christians" believes (*The Next Christendom*, 3).

8. Lamin Sanneh, *Whose Religion Is Christianity? The Gospel beyond the West* (Grand Rapids, MI: Eerdmans, 2003), 28. Following references will be noted parenthetically.

9. Lesslie Newbigin, *The Gospel in a Pluralistic Society* (Grand Rapids, MI: Eerdmans, 1989), 244.

10. Daniel J. Wakin, "Where the Gospel Resounds in African Tongues," *New York Times*, April 18, 2004.

11. Mark Gornik, "Signs of the Spirit in the City," www.livedtheology.org.

12. Mark Gornik, an interview with the author.

13. Albert J. Raboteau's "American Salvation: The place of Christianity in public life," *Boston Review* (Spring, 2005).

14. Ibid.

15. Mark Gornik, an interview with the author.

16. Most white evangelicals did not pray for Bill Clinton, we should recall; they hated him. At the 1999 National Prayer Breakfast, which took place during the height of the Clinton impeachment proceedings, I sat next to the owner of a large department store chain, who was also a board member of the Billy Graham Evangelistic Association. When the president and first lady appeared on the stage, and the three thousand attendees stood to their feet out of respect for the office, the evangelical leader said gruffly, "I am not standing up for that ole slick Willy." He remained in his seat, along with several other self-identified evangelicals at the table, including one who had earlier in the program become emotionally transported during Michael W. Smith's praise song, raising her hands in the posh ballroom of the Washington Hilton and Towers, which preceded the president's talk.

17. Reverend Dr. Robert Marsh, correspondence with the author.

18. Historical Commission of the Southern Baptist Convention, Nashville, Tennessee.

19. Karl Barth, *Against the Stream*, 16.

20. N. T. Wright, "That Special Relationship," *The Guardian*, October 18, 2003.

21. John Calvin, *Institutes of the Christian Religion*, vol. I, 183.

22. Ibid., 202.

23. Cf. "The Land Letter," October 3, 2002, http://en.wikisource.org/wiki/Land_letter.

24. Steven Strang, "The Faith of George W. Bush," *Charisma*, October, 2003; "An Inaugural Moment," *Charisma*, March, 2005.

25. David P. Gushee, "5 Reasons Why Torture is Always Wrong," *Christianity Today*, February, 2006.

Chapter Nine

1. Bonhoeffer, *Letters and Papers from Prison*, 3–17.

2. The best account of the rise and fall of the Confessing Church is Victoria J. Barnett's, *For the Soul of the People: Protestant Protest against Hitler* (New York: Oxford University Press, 1992).

3. Dietrich Bonhoeffer, *Ethics* (New York: Macmillan, 1955), 181.

4. Dietrich Bonhoeffer, *Letters and Papers from Prison*, 337.

5. Ibid., 16.

6. Padilla and Scott, *Terrorism and the War in Iraq*, 34. On the difficulty of sustaining a robust theological critique amidst the myriad diversion of corporate capitalism, I recommend Eugene McCarraher's marvelous book, *Christian Critics: Religion and the Impasse in Modern American Social Thought* (Ithaca, NY: Cornell University Press, 2000).

7. Martin Luther King Jr., *A Testament of Hope: The Essential Writings and Speeches of Martin Luther King, Jr.* (San Francisco: HarperSanFrancisco, 1990).

8. Padilla and Scott, *Terrorism and the War in Iraq*, 34.

9. Ibid.

10. Dietrich Bonhoeffer, *Letters and Papers from Prison*, 337.

11. Augustine, *Confessions*, 296.

12. D. Massimo Lorenzini, "Taking Every Thought Captive," Frontline Ministries, www.frontlinemin.org/truth.asp.

13. The quote has long been attributed to Luther, though it may be apocryphal.

14. Wright, "That Special Relationship."

15. For example, during the Clinton impeachment imbroglio of 1998, more than 140 theologians, religious leaders, and scholars signed a stinging rebuke of the president's sexual misconduct and perjurious testimony. The document, which was eventually published and expanded in a book entitled *Judgment Day at the White House*, criticized the president for his appearance at a prayer breakfast on September 11, 1998, where he acknowledged moral wrongdoing and asked forgiveness of the ministers. While most of the participants of the prayer breakfast accepted the president's apology, the theologians, religious leaders and scholars who drafted the so-named "Declaration Concerning Religion, Ethics, and the Crisis in the Clinton Presidency" regarded Clinton's appeal as a "political misuse of religion and religious symbols" and his repentance as "incomplete."

   One dissenting theologian, Lewis Smedes of Fuller Theological Seminary, responded to the Declaration by answering William Bennett's question, "Where is the outrage?" by saying: "I am outraged at how Bennett's friends in Congress predictably bow their knees to the National Rifle Association whenever guns are an issue. I am outraged that no President since Lyndon Johnson has had the courage to keep before our conscience the black smog of poverty that chokes all hope out of the people who live in our inner cities. I am fiercely angered, shamed, and deeply disappointed by Bill Clinton—but not quite outraged. Outrage I leave to the saints, the scholars, and the Christian Coalition." Another dissenting voice, the Christian philosopher Nicholas Wolterstorff, questioned the very premise of the "Declaration," namely, that Clinton remained unrepentant, since Clinton had, in fact, confessed his wrongdoings and asked forgiveness at the prayer meeting. Tellingly, no petition would be drafted by these same outraged men and women to challenge the unapologetic decisions of the president who led the nation into war on false premises and under the banner of Christian duty.

16. Thomas Merton, *Faith and Violence* (South Bend, IN: University of Notre Dame Press, 1968), 142–143.

17. King cited in Taylor Branch, *Pillar of Fire* (New York: Simon & Schuster, 1998), 30.

BIBLIOGRAPHY

Athanasius. *The Life of Antony and the Letter to Marcellinus*. Translated and edited by Robert C. Gregg. New York: Paulist Press, 1979.

Augustine. *Confessions*. Translated by Henry Chadwick. Oxford: Oxford University Press, 1991.

Balmer, Randall. *Thy Kingdom Come: How the Religious Right Distorts the Faith and Threatens America*. New York: Basic Books, 2006.

Balthasar, Hans Urs von. *Dare We Hope That All Men Be Saved?* Translated by David Kipp and Lothar Krauth. San Francisco: Ignatius Press, 1988.

Barth, Karl. *Against the Stream: Shorter Post-War Writings, 1946–1952*. New York: Philosophical Library, 1954.

———. *Church Dogmatics*. Translated by G. W. Bromiley. Edinburgh: T&T Clark, 1961.

———. *The Humanity of God*. Richmond, VA: John Knox Press, 1960.

———. *The Word of God and the Word of Man*. Translated by Douglas Horton. Gloucester, MA: Peter Smith, 1978.

Barton, Ruth Haley. *Invitation to Solitude and Silence: Experiencing God's Transforming Presence*. Downers Grove, IL: InterVarsity Press, 2004.

Benjamin, Walter. *Illuminations: Essays and Reflections*. Edited by Hannah Arendt. Translated by Harry Zohn. New York: Schocken Books, 1968; originally published 1955.

Birch, Bruce C. *What Does the Lord Require? The Old Testament Call to Social Witness*. Philadelphia: The Westminster Press, 1985.

Bivins, Jason C. *The Fracture of Good Order: Christian Antiliberalism and the Challenge of American Politics*. Chapel Hill: The University of North Carolina Press, 2003.

Blumhardt, Christoph. *Action in Waiting*. Farmington, PA: The Plough Publishing House, 1998.

Bonhoeffer, Dietrich. *Discipleship*. Translated by Barbara Green and Reinhard Krauss. Minneapolis: Fortress Press, 2001.

―――. *Ethics*. New York: Macmillan, 1955.

―――. *Letters and Papers from Prison*. New York: Macmillan, 1972.

―――. *Life Together*. Translated by John W. Doberstein. San Francisco: Harper & Row, 1954.

Budde, Michael. *The (Magic) Kingdom of God: Christianity and Global Industries*. Boulder, CO: Westview Press, 1997.

Calvin, John. *Institutes of the Christian Religion*. Edited by John T. McNeill. Translated by Ford Lewis Battles. Philadelphia: The Westminster Press, 1960.

Campbell, Will D. *Brother to a Dragonfly*. New York: Seabury, 1977.

Camus, Albert. *The Rebel: An Essay on Man in Revolt*. Translated by Anthony Bower. New York: Vintage Books, 1991.

―――. *Resistance, Rebellion, and Death*. Translated by Justin O'Brien. New York: Alfred A. Knopf, 1961.

Carter, Jimmy. *Our Endangered Values: America's Moral Crisis*. New York: Simon & Schuster, 2005.

Cochrane, Arthur C. *The Mystery of Peace*. Elgin, IL: Brethren Press, 1986.

Connolly, William E. *Why I Am Not a Secularist*. Minneapolis: University of Minnesota Press, 1999.

Davies, Alan. *Infected Christianity: A Study of Modern Racism*. Kingston, ON: McGill-Queen's University Press, 1988.

De Gruchy, John W. *Christianity and Democracy: A Theology for a Just World Order*. Cambridge: Cambridge University Press, 1995.

De Lange, Frits. *Waiting for the Word: Dietrich Bonhoeffer on Speaking about God*. Translated by Martin N. Walton. Grand Rapids, MI: Eerdmans, 1995.

Dunbar, Anthony. *Against the Grain: Southern Radicals and Prophets, 1929–1959*. Charlottesville: University Press of Virginia, 1981.

Ellul, Jacques. *The Humiliation of the Word*. Translated by Joyce Main Hanks. Grand Rapids, MI: Eerdmans, 1985.

Fiumara, Gemma Corradi. *The Other Side of Language: A Philosophy of Listening.* London and New York: Routledge, 1990.

Gornik, Mark. "New Centers of Scholarship: Andrew Walls on World Christianity and Theological Education." *The Princeton Theological Review* volume XL, 2: 9–12.

———. *To Live in Peace: Biblical Faith and the Changing Inner City.* Grand Rapids, MI: Eerdmans, 2002.

Gorringe, Timothy. *The Education of Desire: Towards a Theology of the Senses.* Harrisburg, PA: Trinity Press, International, 2002.

———. *Karl Barth: Against Hegemony.* Oxford: Oxford University Press, 1999.

Guardini, Romano. *Prayer in Practice.* Translated by Prince Leopold of Loewenstein-Wertheim. Garden City, NY: Image Books, 1963.

Hauerwas, Stanley. *With the Grain of the Universe: The Church's Witness and Natural Theology.* Grand Rapids, MI: Brazos Press, 2001.

Havel, Václav. *Living in Truth.* London: Faber & Faber, 1987.

Hays, Richard B. *The Moral Vision of the New Testament: A Contemporary Introduction to New Testament Ethics.* San Francisco: HarperSanFrancisco, 1996.

Hunsinger, George. *Disruptive Grace: Studies in the Theology of Karl Barth* (Grand Rapids, MI: William B. Eerdmans, 2000.

Irenaeus. *Against Heresies.* Edited by Alexander Roberts and James Donaldson. Grand Rapids, MI: Eerdmans, 1989.

Jenkins, Philip. *The Next Christendom: The Coming of Global Christianity.* New York: Oxford University Press, 2002.

Kavanaugh, John F. *Following Christ in a Consumer Society: The Spirituality of Cultural Resistance.* New York: Maryknoll, 1992.

Kelly, Thomas R. *A Testament of Devotion.* San Francisco: HarperSanFrancisco, 1992.

King, Martin Luther Jr. *A Testament of Hope: The Essential Writings and Speeches of Martin Luther King, Jr.* Edited by James M. Washington. San Francisco: Harper, 1986.

Kirk. K. E. *The Vision of God: The Christian Doctrine of the Summum Bonum.* New York: Harper Torchbooks, 1931.

Leech, Kenneth. *Experiencing God: Theology as Spirituality.* San Francisco: Harper & Row, 1985.

The Liturgy of the Hours, according to the Roman Rite; volumes I-IV. New York: Catholic Book Publishing Company, 1975.

The Lives of the Desert Fathers: The Historia Monachorum in Aegypto. Translated by Norman Russell. London & Oxford: Mowbray, 1981.

Luther, Martin. "The Pagan Servitude of the Church." In *Martin Luther: A Selection from His Writings,* edited by John Dillenberger, 249–362. New York: Anchor Books, 1958.

Malesic, Jonathan Jay. "Disciplines of the Secret: Concealing and Revealing Religious Knowledge in Kierkegaardian Ethics and Fourth-Century Christian Initiation Rites." Doctoral Dissertation, University of Virginia, 2004.

Marcuse, Herbert. *One–Dimensional Man: Studies in the Ideology of Advanced Industrial Society.* Boston: Beacon Press, 1964.

Marsh, Charles. *The Beloved Community: How Faith Shapes Social Justice, from the Civil Rights Movement to Today.* New York: Basic Books, 2005.

Martyn, J. Louis. *Galatians.* New York: The Anchor Bible Dictionary, 1997.

———. *Theological Issues in the Letters of Paul.* Nashville: Abingdon Press, 1987.

McCarthy, David Matzko, and Jennifer A. Lucas. "War Is Its Own Justification: What Americans Think about War," *Political Theology* 6.2 (2005): 165–92.

McCullough, Donald W. *The Trivialization of God: The Dangerous Illusion of a Manageable Deity.* Colorado Springs: Navpress, 1995.

Merton, Thomas. *The Sign of Jonas.* New York: Harcourt, Brace, & Company, 1953.

———. *Faith and Violence.* South Bend, IN: University of Notre Dame Press, 1968.

————. *Raids on the Unspeakable*. New York: New Directions Publishing Corporation, 1966.

Moltmann, Jürgen. *Theology of Hope*. Translated by James W. Leitch. New York: Harper & Row, 1967.

Muers, Nancy. *Keeping God's Silence: Towards a Theological Ethics of Communication*. Cambridge: Cambridge University Press, 2005.

Nelson, F. Burton. "The Relationship of Jean Lasserre to Dietrich Bonhoeffer's Peace Concerns in the Struggle of Church and Culture." *Union Seminary Quarterly Review*, vol. 8, 1–2 (1985): 71–84.

Nelson-Pallmeyer, Jack. *Saving Christianity from Empire*. New York: Continuum, 2005.

Nietzsche, Friedrich. *The Antichrist*. Translated by Anthony M. Ludovici. Amherst, NY: Prometheus Books, 2000; originally published 1888.

Neumark, Heidi, "Strangers No More." In *Getting on Message: Challenging the Christian Right from the Heart of the Gospel*, edited by Peter Laarman. Boston: Beacon Press, 2006.

Padilla, C. René, and Lindy Scott. *Terrorism and the War in Iraq: A Christian Word from Latin America*. Buenos Aires: Kairos Ediciones, 2004.

Pascal, Blaise. *Pensées*. Translated by W. F. Trotter. New York: The Modern Library, 1941.

The Philokalia. Translated by G. E. H. Palmer, Philip Sherrard, and Kallistos Ware. London: Faber and Faber, 1979.

Picard, Max. *The World of Silence*. Translated by Stanley Godwin. Wichita, KA: Eighth Day Press, 2002; originally published 1948.

Pieper, Josef. *Leisure, the Basis of Culture*. Translated by Gerald Malsbary. South Bend, IN: St. Augustine's Press, 1998; originally published 1948.

————. *The Silence of St. Thomas*. Translated by John Murray, S.J., and Daniel O'Connor. South Bend, IN: St. Augustine's Press, 1999; originally published 1953.

Plant, Stephen. *Bonhoeffer*. London: Continuum, 2004.

Rowland, Christopher. *Radical Christianity: A Reading of Recovery*. Cambridge, UK: Polity Press, 1988.

Sanneh, Lamin. *Whose Religion Is Christianity? The Gospel beyond the West*. Grand Rapids, MI: Eerdmans, 2003.

Schmemann, Alexander. *For the Life of the World*. Crestwood, NY: St. Vladimir's Seminary Press, 1998.

Sokolowski, Robert. *The God of Faith and Reason: Foundations of Christian Theology*. Notre Dame, IN: University of Notre Dame Press, 1982.

Stott, John R. W. *Christian Counter-Culture: The Message of the Sermon on the Mount*. Downers Grove, IL: InterVarsity Press, 1978.

Tutu, Desmond Mpilo. *No Future without Forgiveness*. New York: Doubleday, 1999.

Wallis, Jim. *God's Politics: A New Vision for Faith and Politics in America*. San Francisco: Harper, 2005.

Williams, Rowan. *On Christian Theology*. Oxford: Blackwell Publishers, 2000.

———. *Resurrection*. New York: The Pilgrim Press, 1970.

———. *The Wound of Knowledge: Christian Spirituality from the New Testament to St. John of the Cross*. Cambridge, MA: Cowley Publications, 1979.

Wolterstorff, Nicholas. *Until Justice and Peace Embrace*. Grand Rapids, MI: Eerdmans, 1983.

Yoder, John Howard. *The Christian Witness to the State*. Scottsdale, PA: Herald Press, 2002.

———. *Karl Barth and the Problem of War*. Nashville: Abingdon Press, 1970.

INDEX